Anglet ⦿ Bayonne
ean-de-luz ⦿ Biarritz
oure Arcanques
rribia LABOURD ⦿ Urt
Espelette
Sare Ainhoa Cambo-
les-Bains

F R A N C E

Bidasoa R.

B A S S E
N A V A R R E ⦿ Mauléon
St.-Etienne-de-Baïgorry
Irouleguy St.-Jean-Pied-de-Port B É A R N
Ascarat S O U L E

GORGES DE
KAKOVETTA

⦿ Pamplona (Iruña)

N A V A R R A

A R A G Ó N

⦿ Olite

DENAS REALES
ARRA
bro River
⦿ Tudela

N
W E
S

THE BASQUE
COUNTRY

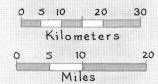

| 0 | 5 | 10 | 20 | 30 |
Kilometers

| 0 | 5 | 10 | 20 |
Miles

THE BASQUE KITCHEN

THE BASQUE KITCHEN

Tempting Food from the Pyrenees

GERALD HIRIGOYEN WITH **CAMERON HIRIGOYEN**

PHOTOGRAPHS BY CHRIS SHORTEN

HarperCollinsPublishers

HarperCollins books may be purchased for educational, business, or sales promotional use. For information please write: Special Markets Department, HarperCollins Publishers, Inc., 10 East 53rd Street, New York, NY 10022.

FIRST EDITION

Designed by Vertigo Design, NYC
Endpaper map © 1999 by David Cain

Library of Congress Cataloging-in-Publication Data
Hirigoyen, Gerald.
 The Basque Kitchen: tempting food from the Pyrenees/Gerald Hirigoyen
 with Cameron Hirigoyen.—1st ed.
  p. cm.
 Includes index.
 ISBN 0-06-757461-0
 1. Cookery, Basque. 2. Food habits—Spain—Pais Vasco. 3. Food habits—France—
 Pays Basque. I. Hirigoyen, Cameron. II. Title.
 TX723.5.S7H53 1998
 641.5946'6—DC21 98-43943

99 00 01 02 03 RRD(R) 10 9 8 7 6 5 4 3 2

To my precious Cameron, whose vision, love, and tenacity ensured that this book would happen—and to Basque people everywhere

CONTENTS

LEFT TO RIGHT: *Tomato Gazpacho with Lobster, Haricots Verts Salad with Figs and Walnut Vinaigrette, Seared Ahi Tuna Steaks with Onion Marmalade, Salmis of Squab Marinated in Red Wine, Veal Loin with Bayonne Ham and Sheep's Milk Cheese, Beet Leaf Fritters, Cherries in Red Wine Soup, Roasted Piquillo Peppers with Fried Garlic Vinaigrette.*

ACKNOWLEDGMENTS

This book, like most, would not have come into existence without the unconditional support and involvement of a wide cast of characters. In our case the participants spanned two continents, and the kinds of support we received ranged from the physical and technical to the emotional and moral—all of which were essential in the completion of this project.

To start, I would like to thank my parents. For it was around their table, back home in the Basque country, that I experienced their love of good food and joy in its preparation, which inspired me to become a chef in the first place.

Maman . . . Merci d'avoir si bien pris soin de ma tenue de cuisinier pendant mon apprentissage, et pour le soutient constant que tu m'as apporté au fil des années et en dépit de la distance qui nous sépare. . . .

There are other friends and family back home to whom I am grateful for their influence on this book.

Peyo, my friend and mentor, for the long nights we spent talking, and for teaching me by example what makes a true restaurateur.

Anita Massol, my sister and friend, thank you for answering my endless questions. *Un grand merci à ma soeur et meilleure amie pour son aide et pour avoir répondu à mes questions sans fin.*

Juan Mari Arzak, whom I fondly consider "the Godfather" of Basque cuisine, for his kind words of encouragement.

Telmo Rodriguez and the entire Rodriguez-Hernandorena family for rolling out a delicious red carpet for us and for their spirited commitment to the region.

Jean Luc Poujauran, for housing our entire clan and for always being there when I've needed him.

Pascal Arcé, for standing in a cold river and still smiling about it, and for the continual welcome, good humor, and good cooking his whole family has shared with my own.

It is here in the United States, however, that this labor of love really took shape. We would like to recognize certain individuals who poured colossal amounts of energy and passion into this project. Without them, we would never have looked so good. To these people we extend our deepest appreciation:

Penelope Wisner, writer and *sage femme*, for her leap of faith and incredible talent for shaping our manuscript into an intelligible book.

Marcelino Ugalde, head of the Basque Library of the University of Nevada, Reno, for his encyclopedic knowledge and generosity in sharing it with us. His supervision made all the difference.

Susan Friedland, our ace editor, for never letting us get away with anything less than the best.

Fred Hill, superagent *extraordinaire*, for his patience (and even his impatience!) in guiding us through the steep "hills" of the publishing world.

Chris Shorten, photographer, for his eye, his tact, his beautiful photographs, and his friendship.

Sara Slavin, prop stylist, for so perfectly understanding and interpreting our vision.

Kimberly Brent, food stylist, for her enthusiasm and meticulous attention to detail.

Pamela Raley, our good friend, without whose efforts we would never have passed go.

Elisabeth Aguirre at Food and Wines of Spain, for her prompt resourcefulness.

Madeleine Kamman, whose gift to me long ago of an antique Basque cookbook from her personal collection gave me the confidence to tackle this subject in my own way.

Bill LeBlond, for sowing the seeds and still being our friend, even if not our "gardener."

Jean Baptiste Lorda, my partner in Fringale and Pastis, for his faith in me from the start.

The entire staff of both Fringale and Pastis, especially Ray Arbelbide, Isabelle Alexandre, Andre DuFour, Taavi Heinla, Martin James, Panchoa Larreguy, Jean-Marie Legendre, Daniel Maurin, Roberto Murillo, Jeffrey Osaka, and Raymond Yee, all of whom have helped me by keeping the ships afloat while I was immersed in this project.

Thom Walton at Fortune Public Relations, my official, tireless, and omnipresent public relations professional.

Delores Kaller, my mother-in-law, for her unofficial though partisan public relations activism.

Harvey, Gina, and Lee, my physical therapists and trainer, whose ministrations keep me going when my engine is running low.

Briselda Zuniga, our baby-sitter, who stayed many extra hours with our son Bix, so we could work unimpeded as our deadline loomed. *Briselda, Le agradeceremos siempre su amor y dedicación para Bixente, asi permitiendonos de terminar este libro. El la quiere muchisimo igual que nosotros.*

There are still others who, although less directly entwined, played meaningful roles, and we would like to acknowledge their generosity both in spirit and in kind:

Ellen Morrissey at HarperCollins, Bonnie Nadell at Fred Hill and Associates, Martine Pelot, Bridgitte Le Plus at Jan-de-Luz in Carmel, the staff of Jean-Vier Linen Factory in St.-Jean-de-Luz, Brigitte Sandquist, Dr. Judy ("the beet lady") Mikacich, Phyllis Paulson, Queenie Taylor, Angele Goyeneche, Andy Powning at Greenleaf produce, Jordan Bow at Royal Hawaiian Seafood, Chris Fontana at Del Monte Meat Company, and John Cawley and Monica Moisan at Pacific Gourmet; and special thanks to all of our "regulars" at Fringale and Pastis (you know who you are), for your continuous support and your belief in what we do.

Last but most important, we would like to thank our children, Justin and Bixente "Bix" Hirigoyen, for enduring, if not completely understanding, our distraction while we were in the process of writing this book. We love you more than words could ever say.

To know how to eat is to know enough.
—OLD BASQUE SAYING

Whenever I return to the Basque country, I follow a personal homecoming ritual. After arriving at the Biarritz airport, I take the twisting coast road out to St. Martin's Point and the tall, slim, very white lighthouse that presides over the landscape. The waves crash against the cliff face below, throwing a soft mist into the air as I look out over white beaches. Today is clear, the sky a startling, electric blue. Gaily striped cabanas in yellow, blue, and red dot the Grande Plage in front of the Palace Hotel, site of the palace built by Napoleon III for his Spanish empress, Eugénie de Montijo. I can see all the way down the coast and into Spain, to San Sebastián. I take a deep breath of the fresh, salty air that smells like nowhere else in the world and know that I am home.

All of a sudden, I am very hungry for the tastes I've been missing: quickly sautéed thin slices of Bayonne ham and an omelet stuffed with my favorite peppers, *biperrak*. These are my comfort foods. I can hardly wait to eat a bowl of small, tender Atlantic mussels in St.-Jean-de-Luz. I will stroll San Sebastián's old town with its hundreds of small bars and restaurants where the savory smells of *pintxos* (the local name for tapas) spill into the narrow, crowded streets. The rest of my family will all follow the same itinerary, individually tailored to our appetites and mood, as we wander from bar to bar, scuff the fresh sawdust that covers the floors, and order glasses of *txakoli*—a crisp, lightly pétillant white wine—and small ramekins of tiny stuffed squid cooked in their own ink. Then I will follow my nose to another bar, order another glass of wine, and perhaps have a wedge of Idiazabal, a smoked mountain sheep's milk cheese.

For dinner tonight, I will take my mother to Madame Hou's simple seafood restaurant, Pantxua, for sautéed fresh anchovies and a big bowl of *ttoro*, the bouillabaisse of the Basque country, and finish off the meal with *mamia*, sheep's milk custard. Her restaurant is decorated with wonderful paintings of Basque country life by Ramiro Arrue. Arrue lived and painted in and around St.-Jean-de-Luz. Since his death in 1971, his art has been rediscovered. During his last years, when he lived alone except for his cat and his work was out of fashion, he often paid for his meals at local restaurants with his paintings.

The next morning when I walk into San Sebastián's fish market and see the glistening displays, I want to buy everything at once! Langoustine, sole, hake, squid, fresh tuna, spider crab, salmon, sardines, and anchovies snuggle in seaweed beds arranged on slanting marble counters.

Nowhere else in the world could there be such a vast, exciting choice of top-quality fish. No wonder Basque chefs have a reputation as the best seafood cooks in Europe. Everyone, from housewives to top-flight chefs, shops at this market. The same quality is equally available to all. I begin to plan lunch around the silvery sardines that have just come into season.

As I sit in a café after shopping, the scent of lemon served with a grilled fish at the next table mingles with the slap of water against the hulls of the red, green, and blue fishing boats. The Basque flags snap crisply in the sea breeze. None of what surrounds me is a folkloric re-creation for the benefit of summer tourists: the men wearing black berets or *txapelas,* the women mending a sea of colorful fishing nets, the half-timbered houses with red- and green-painted trim, the thwack of a *pelota* ball hitting the *frontón,* the Basque street and shop signs, the letters a bewildering jumble of *x*'s, *z*'s and *k*'s. This is a country that lives the rhythms and traditions of the past in the present. Basques are, I believe, deeply involved in rediscovering the power and integrity of our ancestral roots.

EUSKAL HERRIA: THE LAND OF THE BASQUES

Before God was God, before boulders were boulders,
the Basques were Basques. —BASQUE SAYING

When people hear my French accent, they often ask where I am from. If I answer that I am Basque, the response may be a look of incomprehension. Or they say, "Oh, isn't that somewhere around France or Spain? I think I've heard of it. Are they fighting for independence or some-

thing?" The answer is "Yes, it's in France. And yes, it's in Spain. And yes, some Basques are still fighting for independence."

The Basque country straddles the Pyrenees at the throat of the Iberian Peninsula on the Atlantic side. It contains every kind of landscape: mountains, sea, rushing rivers, deep gorges, green pastures, arid plains. The fossil record, carved pebbles, cave paintings, Bronze Age stone monuments called dolmens, and Iron Age cromlechs—circles of standing stones—testify that this region has been continuously inhabited by humans for hundreds of thousands of years.

When Basques arrived in the Pyrenees, how they got there, and how their language developed confound researchers. Despite at least 5,000 years of history, the origin of the Basque people and their language remains a mystery. DNA testing shows the Basques

Outside Sare.

to be distinct from Indo-Europeans, and scholars have been unable to link their language, *Euskara*, to any known language. Romans arriving in the area in the second century B.C. encountered an unknown people, speaking a strange language, whose character was already well formed: taciturn, peaceable, stubborn, brave, and independent. The Romans had found the Basques.

The relationship between the Romans and the Basques foreshadowed relationships the Basques would form thereafter with outside cultures. Roman colonization surrounded the Basque country; other than some mining and the building of roads, the Romans appear to have left the Basques alone, and the two cultures coexisted peacefully.

A definition of the Basque country, if such a thing is possible at all (Basques tend to frustrate generalizations), has rarely been based on political or geographical boundaries. In fact, Basques have experienced political unity for only about 300 years of their long history, in the ninth, tenth, and eleventh centuries under the kings of Navarra. Basque "borders" are based instead on ethnicity and the extent of the territory in which Basque has historically been spoken.

The old stories—with so few facts, Basques rejoice in stories—say that while history in the form of nation-building passed over the plains, the Basques were content to retreat to their mountains to sing and dance. Until the twentieth century, Basques remained unconcerned with political structures larger than their regional and town councils. Nor have they been interested in the acquisition of territory. As superb long-distance fishermen and explorers from ancient times, Basques had many opportunities to claim new lands. But they did not. Instead, they appear to have applied a fisherman's perspective to solid land: that one can enjoy the fruits of the sea, but the sea itself cannot be owned.

The rugged Pyrenees and Cantabrian mountains have protected and isolated the Basques from other peoples and, until the advent of better roads and modern methods of communication, from each other. Because the mountains separated Basques into small villages, the style of government they developed was a rough sort of community-based democracy. It is characteristic of the Basques that the individual could not vote on the village council. Instead, the "house" voted. Each family occupied a house and their designee would vote. The house became so important that each was given a name. Even today you will see the house name carved over the front door. Anyone living in the house came to be known by the name of the house.

The Basque *fueros* (village councils and charters) structured community life. They regulated items as diverse as the planting space required between apple trees, local taxes, and the date the sheepherders would take their flocks up to the commonly owned mountain pasturage, as well as the lending of fire to anyone whose hearth had been extinguished. Before Basques would recognize any political authority superior to their local governments, these rights, which included freedom from outside taxation and conscription, had to be sustained. The defense of these traditional privileges and the way of life they represent continue to define Basque culture and to motivate Basques to strive for autonomy from any nation-state claiming control of the Basque country.

The Basques occupy a strategically important landscape. The Pyrenees at their highest rise about 11,000 feet but are almost impassable except along the Atlantic and Mediterranean coasts. Since the Basques control the western mountain passes and the coastline of the Bay of Biscay, they have stood in the path of invading armies from the north and south, including Romans, Visigoths, Muslims, the Holy Roman Empire, and the English, French, and Spanish.

The goal of those armies was not Basque territory itself but the lands and capital cities that lay beyond. In exchange for guarantees of autonomy, Basques would allow the armies to pass unmolested through their country. In the eighth century, Charlemagne, frustrated in his attempt to oust the Muslims from the Iberian Peninsula, turned aside to attack the Basque city of Pamplona and destroyed its walls. In retaliation, the Basques pounced on his rearguard and annihilated it. A thousand years later, the Basques aided Napoleon in his conquest of Spain in exchange for his promise to unite all of the Basque country and grant it autonomy. He did not keep his promise, however.

Early in the eleventh century, Sancho the Great of the kings of Navarra consolidated all of the Basque territory with Castile and part of Aragon. Forty years later, he redivided the United Kingdom of Navarra among family members, creating smaller kingdoms of Navarra, Aragon, and Castile, and two viscountcies, Labourd and Soule. Internecine battles and marriages transferred control of the now-separate regions from one to another, to England, France, and back, until in the fifteenth century, the smaller, agricultural provinces to the north of the Pyrenees became part of France and those lying to the south and west were united under the Spanish crown.

Soon after their creation, Labourd and Soule came under the control of Aquitaine, and then, through the marriage of Eleanor of Aquitaine to Henry Plantagenet, they passed to the English crown. Charles VII of France and Joan of Arc, whose standard-bearer was called "the Basque," defeated the English in 1451. Labourd and Soule then became, and stayed, part of France.

To the south, the Basques of Alava, Biscay, and Guipúzcoa peacefully aligned themselves with Castile. In the thirteenth century, they then lent armies to the King of Castile in his quest to conquer Navarra. This was probably the first, but not the last, time Basques would fight each other. Repercussions of the mistrust sown then may account for the separate courses Navarra and the other Spanish provinces would follow even into the twentieth century.

The smaller states created by the breakup of the united, ancient Basque kingdom of Navarra form the basis for the current seven Basque provinces. The international French-Spanish border further divides the country. Three provinces lie on the French side of the border:

Pamplona (Iruña).

Labourd hugs the coast; Basse Navarre, once part of Navarra in Spain, lies to the south of Labourd; and the wild, isolated Soule is further south and east.

On the Spanish side, with five times the population and ten times the land mass, the divisions are even more complicated. The French-Spanish border forms the boundary between the French provinces and its neighboring province to the south, Navarra. It is the largest Spanish Basque region and stretches from a few miles of the coast to deep within the dry, hot central plains of Spain. Navarra has been granted limited independence by the Spanish government, and Pamplona is the capital. Guipúzcoa lies in the middle of the Basque country on the coast, and San Sebastián is its best-known town. Vizcaya (Biscay) and its capital, Bilbao, hold the western extremity while, to the south, Alava borders both Vizcaya and Guipúzcoa. Together, Vizcaya, Guipúzcoa, and Alava make up Euskadi, the Basque autonomous region, endorsed by Spain in 1980.

Accordingly, in the Basque country there are at least four ways to say and spell anything. Take, for instance, "thank you." I could say it in French as *merci*, in Spanish as *gracias*, in *Euskara* on the French side as *mil esker*, or in *Euskara* on the Spanish side as *eskerrik asko!* There is often no agreement between guidebooks and maps on the spelling of place names, confusing tourists and natives alike. Natives of *Euskal Herria* are called *Euskaldunak*, or "people who speak Basque." Never mind that of a total population of approximately 2,800,000 only about 27 percent speak *Euskara* and those, in turn, speak more than eight dialects. This multiplicity results from the isolation caused by the mountainous countryside, by the French-Spanish border, and most importantly, perhaps, because *Euskara* was officially banned in 1937 under Generalissimo Franco's regime, a ban that lasted approximately forty years.

In 1979 a unified Basque dialect called *Batua*, codified by the Basque Language Academy, became, with Spanish, a co-official language of Euskadi, the Basque autonomous region. It is the dialect taught in schools and used by the media, and it is the language used in books published in the native tongue. Neither Navarra nor the French Basque provinces, however, have officially adopted *Batua*.

The complications, divisions, and borders are eroding under the pressure of a reinvigorated economy and a resurgence of Basque nationalism as exemplified by the iridescent, titanium-clad Guggenheim Museum that changes its look with every flash of light. In a reflection of the past when local councils supported public works such as roads, Bilbao entirely funded this powerful representation of Basque pride. In addition, modern methods of transportation and communication have pierced the traditional isolation of the Basque country. Bilbao, for example, is now only a two-hour drive by superhighway from Biarritz. Modern methods are even encroaching on the most ancient of Basque occupations, sheepherding. I laughed out loud when I saw a shepherd working his flock in a Honda Accord!

INDEPENDENCE

Deep in their hearts, Basques share a commonality of spirit and culture that is now expressed more directly than ever. In the 1990s street and shop signs appeared in both Basque and either French or Spanish. And more and more people are sending their children to Basque schools to learn to speak and read the Basque language, which is now officially recognized on both sides of the border. Part of the charm of the Basque country, however, is its deeply rooted regionalism. There is not yet a strong sense of collaboration or cooperation.

This resurgence of Basque spirit is felt with varying degrees of intensity on the French and Spanish sides of the border. Since the Basque provinces of Labourd, Basse Navarre, and Soule were annexed by France more than 500 years ago, they have enjoyed the benefit of a stable, centrally administered government. Unlike their Spanish brothers, French Basques have never experienced a dictator; nor has the French government attempted to stamp out the Basque language or customs. Because the region was small, relatively poor, and agricultural, the government never paid it much attention. Instead, in the mid-nineteenth century it became a royal playground as the courts of Europe followed the emperor Napoleon and his empress Eugénie, to the shore at Biarritz.

Spain, like France, was united in the fifteenth century and included the Basque provinces Alava, Vizcaya, Guipúzcoa, and Navarra. The Spanish, unlike the French, continued to emphasize regionalism, as exemplified by the country's very name at that time: *l'Espagnas*, the Spains.

The village of Urcuray.

Spanish Basques have experienced two periods of repression of their culture and language. The first was during the nineteenth century; the second was under Franco's dictatorship. To protect their traditional autonomy and their Catholicism, the Basques took the part of Don Carlos, heir to the Spanish throne, against the usurper, Isabella, in the Carlist Wars. The Basques were defeated in 1839 and thereafter oppressed by the anticlerical Isabella, who also believed in a central government. The Basques rebelled once more in the 1870s and were again defeated.

The idea of Basque unity and freedom may have been briefly suppressed but reemerged at the end of the nineteenth century in the speeches and writing of Sabino Arana, considered the founding father of the movement for Basque independence.

In 1931 the Spanish Republic replaced the monarchy, and the Basques lost no time in proposing a statute to grant them autonomy. Navarra, in a reflection of its separate history and perhaps still harboring hurt feelings from its defeat 400 years earlier, refused to participate. Its refusal set the stage for opposing Basque positions in the Spanish Civil War, when once again, Basque would fight Basque.

In the midst of the Spanish Civil War, the Spanish Basque provinces of Alava, Vizcaya, and Guipúzcoa were granted autonomy in 1936 by the Spanish Republic. The ceremony took place in Guernica, the symbolic center of Basque culture. Since ancient times, regional councils met under an oak tree in Guernica to decide communal Basque affairs. Over the intervening centuries, monarchs repeatedly journeyed to Guernica to confirm Basque freedoms.

The first act of the new Basque government in the fall of 1936 was to adopt the red, green, and white flag, *ikurriña*, created by Sabino Arana. The red ground represents the people; the green cross symbolizes the law, which is always above the people; and the white cross represents the word of God, which reigns above the law and the people. The flag, originally intended for Euskadi alone, was quickly adopted by all Basques as a potent symbol of freedom.

Because the Republic had affirmed Basque traditional (including religious) freedoms, Vizcaya and Guipúzcoa fought beside the Republicans against Franco. In addition, Vizcaya had refused to sell its iron to Hitler. Alava, more agricultural than Vizcaya and Guipúzcoa and more conservative especially in regard to the Church, split itself off from the newly formed Euskadi and fought with Franco. Navarra also aligned itself with Franco, probably for the same reasons as Alava.

Within a few months of its birth, Euskadi, its flag, and Guernica were to become symbols of another sort. On the twenty-sixth of April, 1937, a market day in Guernica, wave after wave of German bombers swooped low over the town, leveling it and killing 2,000 civilians. It was the first carpet bombing of civilians in history.

Bilbao struggled on alone for almost a year, too far removed from the main theater of the war to be sent much help from the Republic. The city fell in 1937. The frontier closed, and Pamplona went up in flames. Horrified Basques on the French side lined their balconies to watch the fires rage.

Franco then began a long and ruthless suppression of Basque culture. Intellectuals were murdered or disappeared. Newspapers and schools closed. The language and the flag were prohibited. Franco was so thorough that no Basque teachers were allowed to teach in Basque country schools. Any child speaking Basque was severely punished.

As it always has done in the Basque country, repression gave birth to resistance. In 1956, a split in the Basque Nationalist Party gave birth to the ETA militant organization *(Euskadi Ta Askatatuna* or Basque Homeland and Liberty), dedicated to achieving unity and independence for all Basques, in Spain and in France. A similar organization, *Enbata,* came into existence on the French side. Many of the activities of these organizations literally "waved the flag" of Basque independence. Once, when Franco attended the opening day of the annual San Sebastián regatta, he was greeted by the sight of thousands of Basque flags floating in the harbor.

Crossing the border into Spain felt harrowing as recently as the 1960s. The *Guardia Civil* with their stiff, shiny black hats and machine guns were stationed every few yards. One year, my parents and I went to the *Tamborrada*, a festival in the *parte vieja* of San Sebastián that commemorates the tweaking of an occupying army by the village bakers. The story goes that bakers on their way back from fetching water at the village fountain would beat a rhythm on their pitchers in imitation of the drumrolls that dictated the soldiers' changing of the guard. Around this joke has grown a spectacular festival complete with corps of drum-dueling "soldiers" and "chefs," parades, dancing, and feasting. It is also the one day of the year that San Sebastián's fabled gastronomic societies (private dining clubs) open their doors to the public. The year my parents and I attended, the mayor, a member of Franco's party, was scheduled to speak. Before he could begin, the crowd threw tomatoes. Soon riots broke out.

In 1973 ETA assassinated Franco's prime minister, Luis Carrero Blanco. A car bomb sent him and his limousine sixty feet into the air. Franco had also trained the young king, Juan Carlos, to prepare for the restoration of the monarchy. When we received news of Franco's death in 1975, I was eighteen, and I remember we poured into the streets and partied all night.

Juan Carlos shocked the world by not continuing authoritarian rule. Instead, he called for elections and a new constitution. The Basque provinces never ratified the constitution, however, because it did not grant them the level of autonomy they wished. Therefore, they have not felt strongly bound to the central government.

The Basque intransigence over the constitution did not prevent Juan Carlos from pursuing statutes of autonomy for both Euskadi and Navarra. The achievement of autonomous status in 1980 relieved some of the immediate pressure for independence. The installation of a socialist government in Madrid in the 1980s further improved the Basques' position. They achieved their own police force and the freedom to collect their own taxes, sending only a portion to the central government.

Yet you can still occasionally feel tension, especially on the Spanish side. The ETA, though outlawed, continues its fight to achieve unity for all Basques in an independent state and for the release of Basque political prisoners still held in Spanish prisons. One evening recently, my wife and I were walking in San Sebastián when suddenly a group of masked kids rushed by and spray-painted the entire arcade of the old city hall with ETA slogans. While not actually dangerous, the experience was deeply unsettling.

Herri Batasuna, a coalition of many parties, acts in part as a political voice for the prohibited ETA. The current conservative Spanish government has again resorted to repressive tactics in its efforts to control ETA activities. Recently, a major Basque newspaper, *Egin*, was shut down, and a number of *Herri Batasuna* directors have been jailed and others threatened with imprisonment.

It is sometimes unbearable to read the local newspapers, with their reports of terrorist bombings and shootings. Now that Basques man their own police force in Euskadi, suppressing terrorist activities takes on the profoundly troubling stain of brother against brother. The vast majority of the population does not support the ETA. The ETA's actions can have the opposite of their desired effect, hardening the Basques against what they see as immoral acts. Their reaction has fostered the rise of an active peace drive; in the last few years, thousands have marched in peace demonstrations.

St.-Jean-de-Luz harbor.

THE TASTE OF BASQUE CUISINE

The ocean's tidal rhythms that ordain fishermen's lives and the seasonal cycles followed by shepherds and farmers have molded Basque culture and still imprint the cuisine. In an odd reversal, the Pyrenees—mountains that divide nations—form and unite the Basque people. This is inherently a union of opposites: a mountain culture perched on the edge of the sea. For longer than memory, Basques have fished, hunted, herded, and farmed their country. The cooking is still peasant cooking in the best sense: food that remains close to its roots, copious, simple, seasonal, and regionally specific.

Basques who live near the sea eat fish at least once a day, and almost all Basques live close to the sea—or to a river. All Basques, wherever they live, love salt cod. It was Basque whaling fleets chasing their prey across the North Atlantic that discovered great quantities of cod off the Newfoundland coast. When the Catholic Church relaxed its "No meat on Friday" regimen, Basques paid no attention. By then they had created dishes so good they would never give them up; just two of many are Salt Cod "al Pil-Pil" (page 88) and Salt-Cod Stuffed Peppers (page 86).

Fishermen never waited to get ashore for a good meal. As long as the weather remained calm, the men cooked aboard, making simple fish stews and soups of whatever they had on hand. Those dishes jumped ship to become celebrated signature dishes of the region. Within the history of *Marmitako* (Yellowfin Tuna and Potato Stew, page 104), a stew of fresh tuna, potatoes, garlic, onion, and peppers, lies the memory of generations of St.-Jean-de-Luz's tuna fleets.

Sheep are ideally suited to mountainous terrain, and so they have become the animal of choice for Basques who live in the mountains. And almost all Basques live in the mountains, or in mountain valleys, or close to mountains. With year-round rainfall, there is almost always fresh grass for the sheep in either the valleys or the mountain pastures that abound with wild flowers and herbs.

Shepherds continue their seasonal migration, following the good grass up into the communally owned summer pasturage, leaving their families for months on end. They do not, however, leave good food behind. The men cook the succulent young lamb over fires of fragrant wood. They milk their sheep twice a day and make cheese of the rich milk, heating it and cooking the curd in large copper cauldrons balanced over open wood fires. Their cheeses have an intriguing smell of sheep's milk, and the taste is at once lightly pungent, mouth-filling, and scented with the wild, fresh plants that fed the animals.

France has created an AOC (Appellation d'Origine Controllé) status for the cheeses, *Ossau-Iraty*. The purpose of appellations is to identify and protect the quality of regional products. We are probably most aware of the designations in relation to French wines. Spain has a similar system, abbreviated AO. Several Basque sheep's milk cheeses have won AO recognition, including Roncal from Navarra and Idiazabal from Guipúzcoa. Such protection may come at a price, however, because appellation regulations often blend political and economic considerations with traditional production practices. In the case of the French cheese, at least, AOC regulations permit pasteurized milk. Pasteurization is not commonly practiced among sheepherders, who may have no access to a pasteurizer and, in any case, probably have no intention of pasteurizing their milk. These renegades or traditionalists, depending on one's point of view, continue to make their cheese as they always did. Their individual cheeses are more prized than ever by a clientele that wants only the authentic flavor of *ardi gazna* (Basque for sheep's milk cheese).

Jara mountainside.

The expansive mountain pasturage for sheep resulted from the shrinking of the vast forests that once covered much of the Basque country. The combined effects of lumbering, shipbuilding, charcoal-making, and fires devastated the forests. However, thousands of acres remain, especially the Iraty forest on the French side. The forest makes a great habitat for game as well as forage for pigs that happily gobble up acorns and chestnuts. The nuts help create the flavor and fat that mark the best ham, especially that of Bayonne, renowned throughout the world.

Many Basques have traditionally cured their own hams as well as their own chorizo, rillettes, andouille, confit, and pâtés. Pig butchering and the subsequent preparations become neighborly affairs with family helping family and everyone sitting down to huge feasts of fresh pork as the work progresses. Over the years, idiosyncratic seasonings and methods of curing have developed.

The beneficiary of those centuries of refinement is the Bayonne ham. Everything about the ham, from the type of pig to the salt and spices used for curing, comes from close at hand: The pink and black Basque pig, rescued from oblivion, and raised once again specifically for Bayonne ham. Salt from local salt beds. And *piment d'Espelette*, a fruity, piquant, dried red pepper produced in the village of Espelette. Even the fresh, clean air off the Bay of Biscay lends an element to its taste.

Invasions and explorations left in their wake an expanded range of ingredients. The Romans brought wheat, wine, and olive oil. The Muslims introduced rice and citrus. Explorers returned from the Americas with corn, chocolate, tomatoes, peppers, and potatoes. All the routes to the tomb of St. James at Santiago de Compostela converged in the Basque country at St.-Jean-Pied-de-Port, meaning "at the foot of the pass." The care and feeding of thousands of pilgrims—in the thirteenth century, 30,000 a year!—and their preference for wine over the local fermented cider, resulted in the proliferation of vineyards and the building of many monasteries along the route. Jews fleeing the Spanish Inquisition brought their secret knowledge of chocolate making to Bayonne. Chocolate was first a drink, but in Bayonne the chocolatiers discovered how to turn it into a solid, unctuous bar.

Despite such rich abundance, none of the foods that adorn Basque tables can be taken for granted. Basque cuisine consists of food procured by labor and prepared to satisfy the hearty appetites of laborers. The food is hard won by hours or years of work. Even mushrooming— and Basque country is close to heaven for mushroom hunters—sometimes takes hours of walking before a small basket can be taken to market. The one exception might be the abundant crop of chestnuts that fall to the ground each autumn, although getting through their hard jackets is a challenge in itself. This could be why Basques love them so much—chestnuts are as contradictory (hard on the outside and soft and generous within) as the people themselves!

Yet this is a joyous cuisine. Generation after generation has invested heart, soul, and body in the ritualized gestures that create a cheese, or a ham, or a dish of *pipérade*, the Basque classic made of tomatoes, green peppers, onions, and garlic. Basque fishermen take fierce pride in their line-caught squid and tuna. And any Basque buying that squid knows what line-caught means in terms of quality and taste. Without conscious intention, the preparation of Basque cuisine has become a living, evolving celebration of centuries-old traditions.

Basques typically spend twice what an American does on food and far more time in its preparation. Almost any conversation at any time of day will soon turn to food, and political discussions are banned at table to prevent arguments from interfering with enjoyment. A definition of Basque culinary pleasure extends beyond any particular meal. It expands to include the fishermen, sheepherders, farmers, and cooks who provide the food and beyond them to the land itself and the generous sea.

Basques express their appreciation and celebrate their way of life with an active calendar of festivals. Every town and city fêtes its offering to the common culinary heritage. Itxassou celebrates its luscious black cherries. Santurce celebrates its sardines, Espelette its *piments*, St.-Jean-de-Luz its tuna, and Tolosa its shiny black beans. Bayonne recently devoted a whole year of festivities to its chocolate!

Culinary competitions for the best *garbure* or *ttoro* are major attractions of the festivals and provide opportunities for amateur cooks to test their culinary skills. There are organized parades with corps of drummers and *txistu* players. The *txistu* is a flute-like wooden instrument with a sweet sound played in conjunction with a small drum, a *ttun-ttun*. One of my best friends, Xabier, was an especially talented *txistulari*. Whenever he played in the street, people followed him as if he were the Pied Piper. In the evening in the tapas bars a *bertsolari*, a direct descendent of the troubadours, might improvise a rhyming song on the spot. Throughout the day and well into the night, there is often singing and dancing in the street.

One year, when my older son, who was born in the United States, was just a small boy, we attended a festival together. The street was a sea of white-clad people with red sashes at the waist, red kerchiefs at the neck, and red berets on all the men—the national festival costume worn by all Basques. Justin, being American, at first refused to wear such an outfit. But as we walked, I noticed him lagging behind and hanging his head. When I asked what was wrong, he mumbled that he wanted to be dressed like everyone else. We rushed off to get him properly attired, and soon he was happy again.

THE BASQUE MEAL

When there is no festival, Basques will still celebrate. Any meal can create a festive atmosphere. Meals have a leisurely pace and are served in courses. A long table flanked by stools or benches is common in homes as well as in traditional restaurants and *cidreries* (cider-tasting houses) and encourages a casual, friendly atmosphere. Old photographs show whole villages gathered outdoors around such tables laden with food.

When I grew up, both lunch and dinner were important meals comprising several courses. They were served family-style and typically began with soup. Traditional restaurants still serve this way, bringing out a tureen of soup for the whole table and platters of salad and meats.

A vegetable dish such as asparagus or artichokes may follow, or perhaps an omelet cut into wedges, or a salad. The main course, a piece of fish if you are on the coast or perhaps a lamb stew if you are in the mountains, is usually served without accompaniments other than bread for sopping up sauce. Dessert is often cheese served with *membrillo* (quince paste) or cherry preserves.

Sweets are typically eaten separately from the meal, either an hour or so afterward or as a snack in the late afternoon. This is when cafés fill and tables are piled high with beignets, macaroons, meringues, and slices of Gâteau Basque served with large cups of foaming hot chocolate.

Above Cambo-Les-Bains.

For entertaining or for Sunday lunch with the family, more courses are added. There will be an appetizer such as marinated anchovies, then a soup, a vegetable or salad, a fish, and then a meat course. All will be accompanied by wine, the beverage of choice for Basques. Cider, made from the abundant apples, was once the favored drink. Apples and cider have been part of Basque culture so long that Basques are said to have introduced the fruit and its cultivation to Normandy, the French region famous for its apples and cider.

After the meat, cheese and fruit or a dessert such as a crème caramel is served, followed by coffee in small cups and brandy and liqueurs. Then comes a pause, and deep-fried pastry fritters are offered. Before the fritters, perhaps while the table waits for them, the singing begins. Basques are always singing. Once a Basque a cappella group performed in San Francisco and came to our restaurant for dinner. Afterward, they began to sing in their deep, resonant, harmonious style. Half the guests thought a CD had been put on!

A COUNTRY OF GOOD COOKS

Throughout Basque history, events such as building a new shepherd's hut or butchering a pig have been the occasions of small fêtes, feasts prepared for everyone who shared the work. In many of those cases, it was men who did the cooking.

That tradition lives on in a unique culinary institution—*txokos*—the Basque gastronomic societies. These are men-only dining clubs where members gather on an almost daily basis to play cards, share conversation, and enjoy a drink, and especially to cook and eat. The clubs are responsible for creating an enormous number of highly skilled amateur cooks. These cooks provide an educated and passionate audience for local chefs.

Each club has a private membership numbering from several dozen to several hundred. Any club may have members from diverse economic and social backgrounds, but the rule is strict that here none of that matters. Only the quality of the food is considered. Some clubs hire a cook who might be the only woman allowed on the premises. But more and more, the men use their clubs as an opportunity to cook for a group of friends, adding their personal touches to the classic recipes.

The men compete with each other in a friendly way as they show off their culinary prowess. They plan their menus with care, shop, and cook as often as once or twice a week. Even professional

Chefs Juan Mari Arzak and Elena Arzak Espina.

chefs are members of the societies but will probably not cook, preferring, for once, to be on the receiving end of someone else's culinary efforts. Sometimes the chefs pick up an idea or two for their own menus!

The societies started at the end of the nineteenth century in San Sebastián, where they continue to play an important role in the town's culinary life. However, the societies have expanded throughout the Basque country. Although they continue to be male bastions, some clubs have begun to relax the rules enough to allow women at lunch. Basque society has traditionally been segregated. At one time, women occupied the seats in the nave of the church while men sat in the balconies. As long as the men are at their club, the women know where they are. It is also possible that their husbands' culinary skills may spur the wives to even greater efforts in the kitchen.

Even if not a member of a gastronomic society, a man is likely to have a group of friends that he cooks for on a regular basis. I think it can be claimed that all Basque men cook. And all Basque children participate in meal preparation. Since so much time is occupied with meal planning and cooking, my sister and I spent a good deal of time in the kitchen peeling broad beans, plucking chickens, and grinding meat for pâté. I loved to help cook and started with little cakes and chocolate mousse to feed my sweet tooth. I already knew it was fun to eat, and then I discovered it was fun to cook, too. By the time I was eight, I knew I wanted to be a chef.

My family cared a great deal about food. My parents even owned a grocery store for a time. Each morning my father would go to the market and buy the best fruits and vegetables he could find. I would help put away the purchases, and to this day I still love stocking shelves at my restaurants. Both my parents cooked and, though we lived in town, we made our own hams, confit, and sausages and canned haricots verts and asparagus when they came into season.

Not every Basque child grows up to be a chef, but every child, through early experiences like mine, thoroughly learns the tastes, textures, and techniques that form the basics of Basque cuisine. Despite the inescapable "modernization" of Basque daily life, families still make it a priority to eat together, and their children learn the fundamentals of their culture through cooking and eating.

Inevitably, young many young people leave the farms and head for office jobs in the industrial areas of the Basque country, especially around Bilbao, where the majority of the Basque population lives. But "gentrification" has a Basque counterpart. Some young families, determined to preserve the social cohesion inherent in the ancient Basque agrarian culture, have moved back to the *baserri* (farmhouses). They pursue higher levels of quality and international recognition for Basque food products in hopes of maintaining the agricultural character of the land. Their efforts are beginning to bear fruit in the export of the roasted peppers of Lodosa and *piment d'Espelette* and in the growing reputation for quality of Spanish extra-virgin olive oils.

Basque chefs, long reputed to be the best cooks in Spain, have always shown a talent for remaining true to the main component of a dish, adding elements that enhance the flavor without masking or confusing it. Beginning in the 1970s, however, something new began stirring. Until then the standard for aspiring Basque chefs was that of Escoffier, the famous French chef who codified classic French cuisine. Small restaurants serving Basque traditional fare were never affected by such pretensions. Then France's nouvelle cuisine with its emphasis on freshness and lightness influenced chefs to move away from heavy sauces, cream, and butter. The effect of nouvelle cuisine on this new breed of chefs was to encourage them to rediscover the classic dishes on which they were raised!

Chefs such as Pedro Subijana, Juan Mari Arzak, Hilario Arbelaitz, Carlos Arguinano, and Martin Berasategui on the Spanish side of the border and Firmin Arrambide, Philippe Ibarboure, Christian Parra, Gregoire Sein, Pierre Chilo, and Jean-Claude Telletchea on the French side are leading exponents of the "New Basque Cuisine." They bring a fresh sense of creative exploration and professional skills to this reinvention of Basque cuisine. They serve recognizable standards at their restaurants because their Basque customers demand hake in green sauce, seafood soup, and veal and pepper stew. But they will also take gazpacho and add unconventional ingredients such as lobster or *piquillo* peppers and then serve it untraditionally, perhaps as a base for fried langoustines, as Philippe Ibarboure does at his Les Frères Ibarboure restaurant in Guethary in the Labourd province. Or, like Hilario Arbeleitz of Zuberoa in San Sebastián, they might take a homely garbanzo bean soup and turn it into a sublime dish by adding such luxury ingredients as foie gras.

When my partner and I opened my San Francisco restaurant Fringale in 1991, I wanted to present the flavors essential to Basque cuisine, combining foods born of the sea and mountains in a way that maintains the integrity of each ingredient and captures the wholehearted devotion that lies at the heart of Basque cooking. My cooking style unites the recipes I learned by helping my parents in the kitchen, my French-Basque heritage, and my later training in Paris.

I have purposely kept most of the recipes in this book simple and free of complicated techniques, so that the home cook can experience how much taste and flavor can be derived from the combination of a few ingredients. The recipes range from traditional dishes such as Leg of Lamb "Zikiro," Poulet Basquaise, and Gâteau Basque to dishes in the style of the New Basque Cuisine, based on Basque ingredients imaginatively combined such as the Bayonne Ham and Sheep's Milk Cheese Terrine (page 58), Honey-Glazed Spareribs (page 152), and Quince and Goat Cheese Layer Cake (page 190). I have given detailed descriptions of the most important ingredients, and a list of resources can be found in the back of this book. In addition, I have included a "Culinary Guide to the Basque Country," giving the names and addresses of just a few of my favorite restaurants and shops. You will also find addresses for sources of information should you decide to plan a visit.

When I visited the *Pays Basque* recently, I stopped in Paris to see my sister. She cooked a dinner of family favorites, Warm Codfish and Potato Salad (page 84) and Poulet Basquaise (page 120), chicken with tomato, onion, garlic, and peppers. The conversation turned to food, as it always does among Basques. My brother-in-law said he did not understand why Poulet Basquaise was such a venerated dish, not only in the Basque country but throughout France. Whenever he ordered it in a restaurant, it disappointed him. My sister and I jumped to defend our culinary heritage. We explained that the chicken must be excellent, the tomatoes must be in season, and the peppers must be the *piments de pays* of the *Pays Basque* with their particular taste and tenderness. And finally, the dish must be cooked with conviction, with understanding, and with passion. Then it is truly Poulet Basquaise.

Gerald Hirigoyen with childhood friends celebrating in the caves of Sare.

I cannot paint like Ramiro Arrue. Nor can I compose like Maurice Ravel, born in Ciboure; nor write like Pierre Loti, the nineteenth- and twentieth-century author who gave the Basque heart a voice. I can, however, cook. And it is through this book of Basque recipes that I want to communicate my love and deep respect for the country that formed me.

NOTES ON INGREDIENTS

Some of the ingredients that give Basque cooking its unique character are not well known here in the United States. They are, for the most part, available, however, so you can cook authentic-tasting Basque dishes. I describe some of these ingredients here and offer substitutions, if you must. Sources for the ingredients are listed under "Mail-Order Sources" in the back of the book. Also included are some items related to my cooking in particular.

BOUQUET GARNI: A bouquet garni is a basic herb flavoring for the French kitchen. It is best when made with fresh herbs, though I have noticed it dried in supermarkets. The standard bouquet garni is composed of 2 sprigs each of parsley and thyme and two bay leaves tied together with kitchen string and used in soups or stews. When the cooking is complete, the bouquet garni is discarded. One way to create your own style of cooking would be to experiment and devise a bouquet garni of your own, adding perhaps more thyme, or a sprig of marjoram or basil.

BAYONNE HAM: Bayonne ham is a salted, cured, unsmoked ham made according to prescribed methods in and around Bayonne. Great ham must start with the pig. And in 1989, twenty producers in the Aldudes Valley decided to rescue from oblivion the Basque pig, a large-eared, black-and-pink creature. Just twenty-five animals existed when the project began. In 1929 the Basque country supported 150,000 of the pigs. In 1996, only 1,200 animals were raised. The pigs roam the forests foraging for acorns and chestnuts and are fed corn and oats. Once the pigs are slaughtered, the hams are rubbed with salt from the Adour or Salies-de-Béarn and laid on a bed of salt. The salt may be mixed with herbs and spices such as *piment d'Espelette* or garlic. Salting lasts about 10 days; then the hams are tied in muslin bags and hung to dry and cure for a minimum of 10 months. The label "Ibaiona" refers only to hams made by this method from the Basque pigs. Bayonne-style hams are made by similar methods but not from the

same type of pig. Serrano ham is a mountain ham produced all over Spain and similar in flavor to Bayonne ham. Bayonne ham is very expensive, but Basques still consume it with abandon, both on its own and as a key ingredient in many preparations including vegetables, chicken, meat, fish, soups, and stews. Bayonne ham, to date, is not exported to the United States, although a few companies do produce American hams in the Bayonne style. Otherwise, high-quality prosciutto is a good substitute, or you can experiment with unsmoked, cured country hams.

CRUSHED GARLIC: I often call for crushed garlic—whole, peeled cloves crushed lightly underneath the flat of a knife blade. When the garlic cooks for a long time, for instance in a soup or stew, it nearly melts into the dish. Remove the pale green central core of each garlic clove if the garlic will be eaten raw or cooked just briefly.

CHORIZO: Chorizo is a flavorful, fully cured pork sausage. The meat is roughly cut and flavored with dried red pepper. Chorizo from the French provinces is flavored with *piment d'Espelette* while Spanish chorizos are flavored with pimentón (Spanish paprika). The sausage may be mild or spicy depending on the type of dried red pepper used. Some chorizos are smoked before curing but most are not. Originally in Basque country, chorizos were made at home. Every fall a pig would be killed and butchered and its various parts made into ham, confit, bacon, pâtés, and sausages. Now the annual butchering is no longer a necessity but is still often practiced and looked forward to as an opportunity to celebrate with neighbors. The recipe for chorizos varies by family and by region. For instance, Pamplona chorizos may contain some beef, and the meat is finely cut instead of the usual coarse cut. Flavorings vary, but garlic is almost as necessary as the dried red pepper. Other seasonings may include oregano, the pulp of dried red peppers, or coriander seeds. Chorizos are eaten simply sliced, sautéed, or added to soups, stews, omelets, potatoes, and bean dishes. Mexican chorizos are usually chili-hot but are readily available and can be substituted for Spanish chorizo. Look, too, for chorizo made by small, quality producers that are now appearing frequently in the American marketplace.

PIMENTS DE PAYS: How I miss these small, green, tender peppers! Their simple name—country peppers—belies the important place they hold in the cuisine. The ones grown in French Basque country tend to be slim and only several inches long while the peppers that go by the same name on the Spanish side are fatter and longer. They are commonly cooked in *pipérades*, omelets, and salads. The closest pepper I can find in the United States is the Anaheim chile.

PIMENT D'ESPELETTE: During the harvest season in Espelette, in Labourd province, the whole village turns red. The small, red peppers are strung by hand and hung in garlands on the outside of each house to dry in the late autumn sun. They are then dried further in old wood-fired ovens overseen by women who never use temperature gauges but hold their hands in their ovens to test the heat. Then the peppers are ground into a fine, red powder with a sweet, fruity, mildly spicy aroma and taste. In 1967 André Darraïdou, the mayor of Espelette, founded an annual festival in to promote *piment d'Espelette*. Traditionally held on the last Sunday of October, it attracts up to 15,000 revelers to a village of 1,600 people. The festivities include a parade, culinary competitions, and much singing and dancing. Chili powder, even that from mild chiles such as New Mexican chiles, smells and tastes smoky and coarse when compared directly with *piment d'Espelette.* You can substitute sweet paprika or mild chili powder but neither will give the delicate complexity of this spice.

PIMIENTO DEL PIQUILLO DE LODOSA: This is the wonderful, slightly piquant, roasted pepper grown in Lodosa, close to the Ebro River in the south of Navarra province. The interplay of climate, soil, plant, and preparation produce a product with an individual, distinctive flavor. The peppers, smaller than American sweet red bell peppers, are harvested and roasted over beechwood fires, then hand-peeled and jarred in their own juices. Nothing more. These peppers have been granted *"Denominación de Origen"* status by the Spanish government, and each jar or tin will carry a label showing the interlocked P and L logo and the words *"Piquillo de Lodosa."* You can substitute roasted, sweet red bell peppers for *piquillo* peppers with success, especially if you look in farmers' markets and specialty groceries for pimiento peppers with their characteristic pointed tip.

SALT AND PEPPER: In my recipes, I specify kosher salt. It is not as salty as either sea salt or table salt, so it is harder to oversalt foods. It does not have additives—table salt does—and is inexpensive. It may be too coarse for your salt shaker, however, so fill a small container from the large box to keep close at hand by the stove. The amount of salt to call for in a recipe is always tricky. The amounts I specify will season the food to my palate, but you may prefer more or less, so always use your own judgment. If in doubt, use less salt. You can always add more salt, but too much will ruin a dish. If you use table salt, cut my salt amounts by half. Occasionally, I like to use a natural sea salt called *fleur de sel*. It is more expensive than other salts but has an extraordinary mineral and floral taste. I will often sprinkle it on a piece of fresh foie gras, for instance. The salt gives a small bite to the texture as well as adding flavor. Many people do like to watch their salt intake and I happily accommodate my customers who request that their food be prepared without salt. At the same time, I believe correct salting is crucial to the balance of a dish. I also prefer to cook with freshly ground white pepper because it is less visually distracting in the finished dish. Whether you use white or black pepper, it should be freshly ground.

SALT COD: The Basques' love affair with salt cod began as a consequence of their whaling expeditions. The Basques were so aggressive and successful as whalers that, by the fourteenth century, they had to chase their prey to the cold North Atlantic waters around Newfoundland, where they discovered shoals of cod. At the same time, the Catholic church created demand by mandating meatless meals. Inland people quickly came to depend on salted cod. By the second half of the fourteenth century, the primary quarry of offshore Basque fishermen became cod to salt and ship to the markets of Europe.

Salt cod can be purchased in ethnic markets, especially Latin American, Spanish, and Italian, which often have the whole fish and will cut and sell only as much as you need. This is preferable, as you can then specify a piece from the middle or loin of the fish, which is thicker and of higher quality than, for instance, the tail. Salt cod is also frequently sold in a 1-pound box. However, when it is purchased this way, you cannot be sure what part of the fish you are buying. Be sure the salt cod is actually Atlantic cod. In America, *bacalao* has become a generic term for salted fish. If you have doubts, ask to see the box, which will state what the fish is and where it came from. The best salt cod is now produced in Iceland.

The highest-quality salt cod is flexible and moist with almost white flesh and a strong sea smell. It should never be as dry and hard as leather! The more moist the piece, the better. The soaking process is not to rehydrate the fish but to remove excess salt. Some markets may have ready-to-use, presoaked salt cod available. It is worth asking.

To prepare salt cod for cooking yourself, soak it in plenty of cold water for 24 to 48 hours, changing the water at least 3 or 4 times. Sauté a few flakes as the soaking progresses to make sure you do not oversoak the fish. Oversoaking removes all the flavor and gives the fish a mushy texture. The fish should retain a somewhat salty flavor. When the fish is soaked, treat it as fresh and cook it as soon as possible.

SHEEP'S MILK CHEESE: Many sheepherders still make their cheese by the methods of their fathers and grandfathers while others produce milk to be sold to cooperatives. After milking, animal rennet is added and curds form. These are cut, drained, and pressed. The cheese is then molded and may be hand-rubbed with salt or passed through a brine bath. Then the cheeses are aged for a minimum of 2 to 3 months.

Sheep's milk cheeses have an intriguing richness and pungency. The younger cheeses are semisoft while the more aged cheeses become firmer and a little piquant. *Ardi gazna* are the generic Basque words meaning sheep's milk cheese (*ardi* = cheese; *gazna* = sheep). On the French side, the cheese has achieved Appellation d'Origine status and there is even a "*Route de Fromage*" with a guidebook, map, and maroon-colored signs posted along the way. On the Spanish side both Roncal and Idiazabal have achieved the equivalent from the Spanish government. Idiazabal is often smoked over fires of beech, hawthorn, cherry, and oak, giving the cheese a complex, smoked taste and an identifiable orange rind.

The AOC status allows pasteurized milk, which is not traditional. Many cheesemakers continue to use unpasteurized milk. These cheeses must be sought out from individual producers or from their wives and daughters who bring them to the weekly markets.

In the United States, you can find the *P'tit Basque*, a mild semisoft cheese; the *Tomme de Pyrénées*, with a slight bite to its flavor and a firmer texture that is appropriate for grating; and more rarely the Idiazabal. I have noticed that the sheep's milk cheese selection is expanding in markets here, and I encourage you to taste several cheeses and choose one or more for your cooking. Dry Jack, a cow's milk cheese, such as the one from Vella in Sonoma, California, would

CHESTNUT SOUP WITH SAUTÉED APPLE

Gaztaina eta Sagar Salda

Tall, glorious chestnut trees grow throughout the Basque country and once upon a time their nuts provided a basic food source. They were even ground into flour to make bread. Their use is more limited now, but you will see chestnuts made into soup or served as a puree with poultry and game. To my palate, celery brings out the best in chestnuts, and I've used a good amount of gently sautéed celery and onion to form a base for this soup. To enhance the flavor further, you might want to sprinkle celery salt on the soup just before serving. The sautéed crisp apple lightens the texture while adding a touch of sweetness. Serve a small bowl of this soup before a stew such as the Civet of Wild Boar (page 130).

SERVES 6 TO 8

- ½ cup plus 1 tablespoon olive oil
- 3 cups coarsely chopped onions
- 4 cups coarsely chopped celery
- 2 pounds unsweetened chestnut puree
- 1 large russet potato (about ¾ pound), peeled and coarsely chopped
- 8 cups Chicken Stock (page 230) or canned low-salt chicken broth
- 1 cup heavy cream
- 1 tablespoon kosher salt
- ½ teaspoon freshly ground white pepper
- 1 tablespoon unsalted butter
- 2 Granny Smith apples, peeled, cored, and cut into ½-inch cubes
- 2 tablespoons brandy
- 2 tablespoons snipped fresh chives

Warm ½ cup olive oil in a small stockpot over high heat. Add onions and celery and sauté for 5 minutes.

Add chestnut puree, potato, chicken stock, cream, salt, and pepper. Bring to a boil and reduce heat to a simmer. Cook, covered, for 40 minutes. Remove from the heat and let stand for 10 minutes.

Working in small batches, transfer the soup to a blender and blend on high speed until smooth and creamy, about 1 minute.

Return soup to the saucepan and bring to a boil. Season with salt and pepper to taste.

In a small sauté pan over high heat warm the remaining 1 tablespoon olive oil with 1 tablespoon butter. When the pan is really hot, add the apples and sauté for 1 to 2 minutes. Add the brandy, and while standing back, set it aflame with a match. Cook until flames die out and apple has lightly browned, 1 to 2 minutes; set aside.

Ladle the soup into shallow bowls. Garnish each with equal amounts of the apple. Sprinkle chives on top.

GARBANZO BEAN SOUP WITH SPINACH AND FOIE GRAS

SERVES 5 OR 6

- 2 cups dried garbanzo beans, soaked overnight in water
- 10 ounces foie gras, cut into ½-inch cubes
- 1 small onion, coarsely chopped
- 1 small carrot, coarsely chopped
- 1 small leek, trimmed and finely diced
- 1 garlic clove, crushed
- 5 ounces unsliced bacon
- 1 cup dry sherry
- 2 quarts Chicken Stock (page 230) or canned low-salt chicken broth
- 1 bouquet garni
- 1 tablespoon kosher salt
- ½ teaspoon freshly ground white pepper
- ½ pound baby spinach

A few years ago I wandered into a bookshop in Biarritz. I could not get into the cookbook section because a man already occupied the narrow aisle. After he left, I started browsing. When I checked out, the cashier noticed my pile of cookbooks and asked me if I knew the man who had just left. "He is a famous Basque chef," she said. "His restaurant is Zuberoa." While I had heard of the restaurant, I had not yet had a chance to go, so I made a reservation that afternoon. My wife and I were smitten from the minute we walked in. The chef, Hilario Arbeleitz, has created an innovative and delectable menu that enhances Basque cuisine without abandoning its roots. Set in a stylish old farmhouse several miles outside San Sebastián, Zuberoa has earned two Michelin stars and has been touted by internationally known food writer Patricia Wells as one of the ten best restaurants in the world. It is run by three brothers: Hilario is the chef, José Mari is the pastry chef, and Eusebio runs the dining room. The last time we were there, we ordered an unusual soup that exemplifies the imaginative way the brothers combine luxury foods with such rustic Basque ingredients as garbanzos and spinach. This recipe is my rendition of that dish.

Rinse the garbanzo beans under clear running water, drain, and set aside.

Place a large saucepan over high heat. When the pan is very hot, add the foie gras, and

sear it until browned on both sides, 30 to 45 seconds. You do not need to add any fat or oil to the pan, as the foie gras will release enough of its own fat when cooking. Remove the foie gras with a slotted spoon and set it aside on paper towels.

Place the same pan over high heat and immediately add the onion. Sauté for 1 minute. Add the carrot, leek, garlic, and bacon and sauté until the vegetables begin to brown, 2 to 3 minutes.

Add sherry and deglaze by stirring and scraping the sides and bottom of the pan to loosen all the browned bits. Add chicken stock, garbanzo beans, bouquet garni, salt, and white pepper. Bring to a boil. Reduce heat and simmer for 1½ hours.

Remove and discard bacon and bouquet garni.

Puree half of the soup in a blender until smooth, then return the puree to the pot. Add the spinach and stir until the leaves are wilted, 1 to 2 minutes. Season with salt and pepper to taste.

Add the foie gras and gently stir the soup just until the foie gras is warmed through.

Serve in shallow soup bowls, taking care to allot some of the foie gras in each portion.

GARBURE

Garbure, a vegetable soup, is such a popular dish in Anglet, a town next door to Biarritz, that it hosts an annual festival in the soup's honor. The event is sponsored by the local *Confrèrie de la Garbure* (Brotherhood of Vegetable Soup).

The members promote the traditions of true garbure to ensure they are carried on by successive generations. A hotly contested cook-off climaxes the festival. Garbure is made in every season, changing its character with whatever produce is available. The fall and winter version features root vegetables. When fava beans arrive in spring, they, too, are added. And in summer the soup contains green beans, tomatoes, and new potatoes. What should remain constant are the ham, white beans, and cabbage.

SERVES 6 TO 8

4 quarts water

2 cups dried white navy beans, soaked in water for 8 to 10 hours

1 bouquet garni

1 pound ham shank

2 medium carrots, coarsely chopped

1 medium celery root, peeled and coarsely chopped

1 medium onion, coarsely chopped

2 medium turnips, peeled and coarsely chopped

1 pound butternut squash, unpeeled, seeded, and chopped into 1-inch cubes

1 small cabbage, cored and sliced into 1-inch-thick strips

3 leeks, trimmed and coarsely chopped

½ cup garlic cloves

2 tablespoons kosher salt

½ teaspoon freshly ground white pepper

10 ounces haricots verts (green beans), trimmed and cut into 1-inch pieces

1 cup cooked, peeled fava beans

Place 4 quarts water, the white beans, the bouquet garni, and the ham shank in a large, heavy-bottomed saucepan over high heat. Cover and bring to a boil. Simmer for 15 minutes, then add the carrots, celery root, onion, turnips, squash, cabbage, leeks, garlic, salt, and pepper. Return to a boil, lower the heat, and simmer, covered, for 30 minutes.

Add the haricots verts and cook until just cooked through, about 10 minutes.

Add the fava beans and cook until they are just warmed through, 1 to 2 minutes.

Remove the bouquet garni and the ham shank. Discard the bouquet garni and reserve the ham shank.

Ladle the soup into individual bowls. If desired, slice the ham and place 1 or 2 slices on each portion. Season with salt and pepper to taste and serve immediately.

TIP: *Garbure is traditionally flavored with the heel of a Bayonne ham, the narrow shank end remaining after the choicest parts have been eaten. In home-cured hams, this includes the bone. The shank is cooked with the soup just until the cook determines it has enough flavor. Then the ham is removed, wrapped, and saved for another use. Hams can be salty, so use care when seasoning your soup.*

CRAB BISQUE WITH BRANDY

When I was a child, I loved to take my little net and chase small crabs called *étrilles* over and around the seashore rocks. When I had captured enough, I took them home to my father, who would turn them into a soup like this one. Here in San Francisco, I use our local Dungeness crabs, but stone or spider crabs will work as well.

SERVES 5 OR 6

3 live crabs (about 1 pound each, or 2 pounds crabmeat)

½ cup olive oil

1 cup brandy

1 cup coarsely chopped carrots

1 cup coarsely chopped onion

1 cup coarsely chopped celery

¼ cup tomato paste

1 tablespoon black peppercorns

¾ cup cornstarch

⅓ cup water

1 cup heavy cream

10 tablespoons unsalted butter

Kosher salt

Freshly ground white pepper

1 tablespoon snipped fresh chives

Pinch of *piment d'Espelette*

Fill a large stockpot three-quarters full of water and bring to a boil. Place crabs in the stockpot and let simmer until cooked through, about 10 minutes. When done, transfer crabs to a cooling rack, and drain the cooking water into a bowl to cool. Carefully remove all of the crabmeat from one of the crabs and set aside.

Remove all of the legs from the remaining two crabs. Using a mallet, crack the legs, and set aside. Remove the outer shell from the crab bodies. Using a large, sharp knife, cut the bodies into quarters.

Warm ½ cup olive oil in the same stockpot over high heat. Add the cracked crab legs and quartered bodies to the pot and sauté for about 5 minutes. Add brandy, carrots, onion, celery, and tomato paste and sauté for another 2 to 3 minutes. Add peppercorns and 12 cups of the crab cooking liquid and bring to a boil. Reduce the heat to a simmer and cook, uncovered, for 1 hour.

Dissolve the cornstarch in ⅓ cup water; set aside.

Strain the soup through a *chinois* or fine-mesh sieve into a large saucepan.

Whisk in the heavy cream, butter, and cornstarch mixture and bring to a boil. Simmer for 10 to 15 minutes. Season with salt and pepper to taste.

Serve in shallow soup bowls. Garnish each with equal amounts of reserved crabmeat, a sprinkling of chives, and *piment d'Espelette.*

LEEK AND POTATO SOUP

Porrusalda

Even though versions of this soup exist all over Europe, *Euskaldunak* (literally "people who speak Basque") think they invented it. It is a staple of home cooking. My family made a huge pot of this soup on Sundays to last the entire week. A portion of soaked salt cod would often be added to cook with the soup for the last 10 minutes or so. If you do add the cod, use care with your seasoning.

SERVES 6 TO 8

- ½ cup plus 3 tablespoons olive oil or Rendered Duck Fat (page 231)
- ½ pound pancetta, sliced ¼ inch thick, then cut into ½-inch squares
- 6 medium leeks, white part only, cut into ¼-inch-thick rounds
- 2½ pounds russet potatoes, peeled and cut into ½-inch cubes
- 1 tablespoon chopped fresh thyme leaves
- 2 bay leaves
- 2 teaspoons kosher salt
- ¼ teaspoon freshly ground white pepper
- 1 small garlic clove, crushed
- 1½ cups ⅓-inch cubes day-old bread
- 2 tablespoons freshly chopped parsley

Heat ½ cup of the oil in a small stockpot over high heat. Add the pancetta and sauté until it begins to release some of its fat, about 2 minutes.

Add the leeks, cover, and cook for 5 minutes, stirring occasionally. Add potatoes, thyme, bay leaves, salt, and pepper. Add enough water to cover, 8 to 10 cups, and bring to a boil, uncovered.

Reduce the heat to a simmer and cook for 20 to 30 minutes. Season to taste.

Warm the remaining 3 tablespoons olive oil and crushed garlic clove in a nonstick pan over high heat. Add the bread cubes and sauté until crispy. Discard the garlic and set the croutons aside on a towel-lined plate. Discard bay leaves before serving.

Ladle into soup bowls and garnish with the croutons and parsley.

POTATO AND WHITE BEAN SOUP WITH OLIVE PUREE

Lursagar eta Babarruntxuri Salda Oliba

This is the traditional soup of Ciboure, a tiny coastal town next to the fishing port of St.-Jean-de-Luz. Originally, the dish was probably eaten for lunch as a mash of beans with potatoes. Now it is served as a thick, creamy soup. The olive puree adds color and a wonderful, unexpected flavor. Olives grow abundantly in the southern Navarra region and are now being made into delicious olive oils.

SERVES 6 TO 8

½ cup olive oil or Rendered Duck Fat (page 231)

1 medium onion, thickly sliced

6 garlic cloves, crushed

1 sprig fresh rosemary

2 cups dried white beans, soaked in water for 8 to 10 hours

2 small russet potatoes (about ½ pound), peeled and coarsely chopped

10 cups Vegetable Stock (page 229) or canned vegetable broth

1 tablespoon kosher salt

¼ teaspoon freshly ground white pepper

25 to 30 Spanish green or Kalamata olives, pitted

Warm the olive oil in a large, heavy-bottomed saucepan over high heat. Add the onion, garlic, and rosemary, and sauté for 5 minutes.

Rinse the beans in a colander under cold running water.

Add the beans, potatoes, vegetable stock, salt, and pepper to the saucepan and bring to a boil. Reduce heat to a simmer, and cook, covered, for 1 hour, or until the beans are soft and tender. Remove rosemary. Season with salt and pepper to taste.

Transfer the soup to a blender and puree on high speed for 1 minute. Return the soup to the saucepan and bring to a boil.

Put the olives in a blender or food processor and mix until pureed. Transfer olive puree to a small squeeze bottle or plastic bag with one corner snipped off.

Ladle the soup into bowls and garnish by squeezing swirls of olive puree on each portion.

ROASTED BELL PEPPER SOUP

Biper Erreta Salda

The roasted peppers give this soup a sweet, smoky flavor. Just enough potato is added to bind the soup without turning it into a potato soup. Until the 1940s, when a long period of scarcity changed the eating habits of even the most resolute, Basques considered potatoes suitable only for animal feed. Now, potatoes appear on Basque tables as often as once a day—from such simple preparations as Fried Garlic Potatoes (page 168) to unusual side dishes such as Potatoes Riojanas (page 170), potatoes cooked with red wine.

SERVES 5 OR 6

½ cup olive oil

1 large onion, coarsely chopped

5 large roasted red bell peppers (page 233), peeled, cored, and coarsely chopped

¼ cup garlic cloves, peeled

2 medium russet potatoes (about ½ pound each), peeled and coarsely chopped

1 tablespoon kosher salt

¼ teaspoon freshly ground white pepper

10 cups Chicken Stock (page 230) or canned low-salt chicken broth

¼ teaspoon *piment d'Espelette*

½ cup crème fraîche or sour cream

1 tablespoon snipped fresh chives

Warm the olive oil in a large saucepan over high heat. Add the onion, roasted peppers, and garlic. Sauté until the onion is lightly browned, about 5 minutes, stirring frequently. Add the potatoes, salt, pepper, chicken stock, and *piment d'Espelette* and bring to a boil. Let simmer, uncovered, until the vegetables are very soft, about 30 minutes.

Working in small batches, transfer the soup to a blender or food processor; puree on high speed until smooth and creamy.

Pour the soup back into the same saucepan. Bring to a boil and season with salt and pepper to taste.

Ladle the soup into shallow bowls. Add a dollop of crème fraîche to each serving. Garnish with equal amounts of chives and a few turns of a pepper mill.

TOMATO GAZPACHO WITH LOBSTER

Otarrain eta Tomate Gazpatxo

Gazpacho originated in Spain's Andalucia and is served throughout Spain, including Basque country on both sides of the French-Spanish border. The ingredients are usually chopped; however, I like to puree the soup with some cooked beet for added color and its subtle, earthy, sweet flavor. The finely diced cucumber and apple add a refreshing touch. Lobster turns this soup into a special-occasion dish, but you could substitute quickly sautéed shrimp. Either way, it is an ideal dish to begin an alfresco dinner or to serve on its own for a luxurious luncheon.

SERVES 6

SOUP

- 3 live lobsters (about 1½ pounds each)
- 3 large vine-ripened tomatoes, cored, peeled, and coarsely chopped (about 2½ cups)
- ½ medium cucumber, peeled, cored, and coarsely chopped (about 1 cup)
- ¼ cup coarsely chopped onion
- 1 large red bell pepper, cored and coarsely chopped
- 4 garlic cloves, crushed
- 1 cup cold water
- ⅓ small cooked red beet (about ½ cup)
- 2 tablespoons sherry vinegar
- 1 teaspoon kosher salt
- ¼ teaspoon freshly ground white pepper
- Pinch of *piment d'Espelette*
- ¼ cup extra-virgin olive oil

To cook the lobsters, fill a stockpot three-quarters full with water and bring to a boil.

Slip the lobsters into the water, cover, and cook until the shells are bright red, about 8 minutes. Using tongs, remove the lobsters. Set aside to cool.

When cool, lay the lobsters on their backs and cut each one in half lengthwise, starting at the head.

Remove and discard the intestinal vein along the back of the tail.

Snap off the claws, crack them with a mallet, and carefully pull the meat out of the shells, intact if possible. Using the same method, remove the tail meat, set it aside with the claw meat, and discard the shells. (Snacking on the rest of the lobster is the cook's bonus for preparing this dish!)

Place the coarsely chopped tomatoes, cucumber, onion, and red bell pepper with the crushed garlic, water, and cooked red beet in a blender; puree until smooth, about 1 minute.

Strain the puree into a bowl using a *chinois* or fine-mesh sieve. Immediately pour the puree back into the blender; add the sherry vinegar, salt, pepper, *piment d'Espelette*, and

¼ cup finely diced apple

¼ cup finely diced cucumber

18 baby red or yellow pear tomatoes, halved

1 tablespoon snipped fresh chives

12 small thin toasts (optional)

extra-virgin olive oil. Blend on high speed until smooth and well combined.

Pour ¾ cup of gazpacho into the bottom of a shallow soup bowl. Place one lobster tail half, cut side up, in the center of each bowl. Prop the meat from one claw up against the tail.

Garnish the bowls equally with the apple, cucumber, tomatoes, chives, and toasts.

SURFERS' SOUP (CABBAGE AND COUNTRY BREAD SOUP GRATINÉE)

Aza Salda Etxe Ogi Xigortuarekin

Hunger is the mother of invention in the kitchen. After a day of surfing—yes, there is great surfing in the Basque country, especially around Biarritz and farther west, in Mundaka, on the coast north of Guernica—a group of us went to a friend's house for a drink. Everyone was starving but when I looked around his kitchen for inspiration, all I could find was a cabbage and a tired loaf of bread. This is a dressed-up version of what I concocted. It's a delicious variation on French onion soup.

SERVES 6 TO 8

½ cup olive oil or Rendered Duck Fat (page 231)

1 large onion, thinly sliced (about 2 cups)

½ pound pancetta, sliced ¼ inch thick, then cut into ½-inch pieces

2 large heads of green cabbage (about 2¼ pounds each), cored and sliced into ½-inch strips

6 garlic cloves, crushed

10 cups Vegetable Stock (page 229) or canned vegetable broth

1 tablespoon kosher salt

¼ teaspoon freshly ground white pepper

1 bouquet garni

½ loaf day-old crusty bread

½ pound grated sheep's milk cheese (about 1 cup)

Warm the olive oil in a large, ovenproof, heavy-bottomed saucepan over high heat.

Add the onion and pancetta and sauté for 5 minutes.

Add the cabbage, garlic, vegetable stock, salt, pepper, and bouquet garni. Cover and bring to a boil. Reduce the heat to a simmer and cook for 40 to 50 minutes.

Cut the bread diagonally into 6 to 8 large slices, about ½ inch thick.

Preheat the broiler.

Remove and discard the bouquet garni from the soup. Season with salt and pepper to taste.

Lay the bread slices on top of the soup, thoroughly covering the surface. Scatter the cheese evenly over the bread.

Place the pot under the broiler until the cheese melts and turns golden brown, 8 to 10 minutes. Remove from the broiler and serve immediately.

WEE HOURS SOUP (GARLIC AND EGG)

Baratxuri eta Arraultze Salda

In the old days, and perhaps even now, sheepherders would make themselves a bowl of this rustic, sustaining soup in the "wee hours" before heading out to tend their flocks. It is also an important tonic for enthusiastic Basque revelers. In a culture that turns a simple dinner into an event where the eating, drinking, and singing can last well beyond midnight, a wedding demands an even greater celebration. This quickly made soup would then be served as a welcome restorative in the early morning hours.

SERVES 4 TO 6

¼ cup olive oil or Rendered Duck Fat (page 231)

10 ounces pancetta, sliced 1 inch thick, then into 1-inch cubes

1 cup diced onion, cut into ½-inch dice

30 garlic cloves, peeled and thinly sliced

2 quarts water

½ teaspoon kosher salt

¼ teaspoon freshly ground white pepper

1 day-old baguette

2 large eggs

Preheat the oven to 400 degrees F.

Warm the olive oil in a heavy-bottomed saucepan over high heat. Add the pancetta and sauté until lightly browned, 3 to 4 minutes. Add the onion and garlic. Sauté until the garlic begins to brown, about 2 minutes. Add 2 quarts water, salt, and pepper; bring to a boil. Simmer for 20 minutes.

Cut the baguette into ½-inch-thick rounds. Place the bread slices on a sheet pan and lightly toast them in the oven. Remove the croutons from the oven and set aside.

Crack the eggs into the simmering soup. Using a whisk, briskly beat the eggs into the soup. Season with salt and pepper to taste.

Place 2 croutons in the bottom of each shallow bowl and ladle the soup over them.

APPETIZERS AND SALADS

EGGS

BASQUE OMELET WITH
BAYONNE HAM   40

ASPARAGUS AND BLACK
TRUFFLE OMELET   42

POTATO AND CHORIZO
TORTILLA   43

IDIAZABAL AND MIXED
PEPPER CROUSTADE   44

PIPÉRADE   46

SOFT-SET EGGS WITH PORCINI
MUSHROOMS AND FOIE GRAS
47

VEGETABLES

ROASTED PIQUILLO PEPPERS
WITH FRIED GARLIC
VINAIGRETTE   48

WILD MUSHROOM RAVIOLI
WITH BLACK TRUFFLE   50

CORN RISOTTO   53

EGGPLANT AND GOAT CHEESE
ROLLS WITH TOMATO SALAD
54

RAGOUT OF ROASTED
VEGETABLES   56

PIQUILLO PEPPER, ROSEMARY,
AND WHITE BEAN GRATIN   57

SPECIALTIES

BAYONNE HAM AND SHEEP'S
MILK CHEESE TERRINE   58

COUNTRY-STYLE PÂTÉ   60

SAUTÉED FOIE GRAS WITH
GRAPES AND VERJUS   61

SEAFOOD

CALAMARI À LA GOULUE   62

ELVERS   63

JUMBO PRAWNS À LA
PLANCHA   64

MARINATED ANCHOVIES   65

SARDINES   66

TUNA CONFIT   68

TUNA TARTARE   69

SALADS

HARICOTS VERTS SALAD WITH
FIGS AND WALNUT
VINAIGRETTE   70

MARINATED TOMATO, ONION,
AND PEPPER SALAD   72

WHITE ASPARAGUS SALAD
73

ROASTED POTATO SALAD WITH
LEMON ZEST AND FRESH
HERBS   74

BASQUE OMELET WITH BAYONNE HAM

Euskal Arroltzemoleta Baionako Urdai Azpikoarekin

This homey omelet is one of the most beloved dishes of the French Basque country. It incorporates two ingredients of which we are fiercely proud, Bayonne ham and *piments de pays*, slim, green, tender peppers grown throughout the country. However, their size, their shape, and even their flavor change according to where they are grown. The smallest, slimmest, and best peppers, to my palate, grow on the French side. They are unlike any other peppers I've tried and are the taste I miss most from my homeland. In the United States I use Anaheim chiles. You will have to go to the Basque country to taste the real thing. Often served sliced into wedges as an appetizer, this omelet could be served for lunch or a simple supper as well.

SERVES 3 OR 4

¼ cup plus 4 teaspoons olive oil

4 medium Anaheim chiles, seeded and finely julienned

Kosher salt

8 large eggs

Freshly ground white pepper

3 ounces thinly sliced Bayonne ham, trimmed of visible fat and finely julienned

1 teaspoon finely chopped fresh parsley

6 to 8 toasted slices of baguette

Warm ¼ cup olive oil in a sauté pan over medium-high heat. Add the Anaheim chiles and a pinch of salt and sauté until lightly browned and very soft, about 9 minutes. Drain and set aside.

Warm 1 tablespoon olive oil in a nonstick skillet over medium-high heat. Whisk the eggs and salt and pepper to taste while the pan is heating. When the oil is hot but not smoking, pour the eggs into the skillet, reduce the heat to medium, and swirl the eggs around a bit. Push the edges in toward the center and shake the pan, keeping the eggs moving until they are evenly set. Scatter the chiles in a line down the center of the eggs. When the eggs are lightly browned on the underside, fold the omelet in thirds, as you would a letter, and slide it onto a serving platter, flap side down. This rolled shape keeps the interior of the omelet warm and moist a bit longer than the "half-moon" shape.

Quickly wipe out the pan, and over high heat combine 1 teaspoon olive oil with the julienned ham. Sauté until just barely warmed through, no more than 20 seconds, then scatter the ham on top of the omelet. Garnish with the parsley and toasts and serve immediately.

TIP: *It is important to sauté the ham in a hot pan right before serving. It needs just a "whisht-whisht-then-out" of the pan or the ham may become rubbery.*

ASPARAGUS AND BLACK TRUFFLE OMELET

This is a terrific spring omelet to serve as an appetizer, brunch dish, or simple but elegant supper. In Basque regions we make one large omelet and serve it cut into wedges. It is far easier to cook one omelet and get it to the table hot than three or four individual ones. A problem may arise if, as happened in my family, someone prefers his omelet soft and another demands a dry one. At home, we solved this dilemma by having Mom and Dad alternate omelet making. His were runny, the way I like them, and hers were firm.

SERVES 3 OR 4

8 large eggs

1 teaspoon kosher salt

¼ teaspoon freshly ground white pepper

2 tablespoons olive oil

16 white or green asparagus spears, peeled, cooked, trimmed to 5 inches, and cut in half if the spears are thick

½ ounce black truffle, finely julienned

1 teaspoon chopped fresh parsley

1 teaspoon snipped fresh chives

In a mixing bowl, lightly whisk the eggs, salt, and pepper; set aside.

Warm 1 tablespoon olive oil in a large nonstick skillet over medium heat. Add the asparagus and truffle, and sauté until the vegetables are hot and the truffle begins to release aroma, 2 to 3 minutes. Using a slotted spoon, transfer the asparagus and truffle to a small bowl.

Add the remaining 1 tablespoon olive oil to the same skillet and place over medium-high heat.

When the oil is hot but not smoking, pour the eggs into the skillet. Reduce the heat to medium, and swirl the eggs around a bit. Push the edges in toward the center and shake the pan some more, keeping the eggs moving until they are evenly set, 2 to 3 minutes.

Distribute the asparagus, truffle, parsley, and chives evenly on top of the eggs. When the eggs are lightly browned underneath, fold the omelet in thirds, as you would a letter, and invert it onto a serving platter, flap side down. This rolled shape keeps the interior of the omelet warm and moist a bit longer than the "half-moon" shape. Season with salt and pepper to taste.

TIP: *Refrigerate the whisked eggs with the truffle overnight in a sealed container. The truffle flavors will permeate the eggs and you will have a truly wonderful dish.*

POTATO AND CHORIZO TORTILLA

I love to roam the old quarter of San Sebastián, stopping first at one bar, then another. By the end of the evening, I will have made a meal from the tempting displays of *pintxos* (the local name for tapas) that include thinly sliced ham, chorizo, marinated anchovies, olives, fried cod balls, squid, and octopus, to name just a few. No bar counter worth its salt, however, is without a tortilla, a Spanish omelet usually made with cubed potato, though the ingredients will vary from region to region. This humble tapa is served in wedges at room temperature. I believe I could live on tortilla and sliced chorizo alone, so I decided to combine them in an omelet that would be a terrific lunch or light supper dish.

SERVES 4 TO 6

⅓ cup olive oil

1 small red onion, finely diced

1 pound Yukon Gold potatoes, quartered or cut in ¾-inch cubes

10 large eggs

1 teaspoon kosher salt

¼ teaspoon freshly ground white pepper

¼ teaspoon *piment d'Espelette*

2 tablespoons chopped fresh parsley

5 ounces chorizo, thinly sliced (about 1 cup)

Preheat the oven to 400 degrees F.

Warm the olive oil in a large ovenproof nonstick sauté pan over medium-high heat.

Add the onion and potatoes, and sauté until the potatoes are cooked through and tender, 14 to 16 minutes.

In a large bowl, lightly beat the eggs together with the salt, pepper, *piment d'Espelette*, and parsley. Add the eggs and the chorizo to the sauté pan and bake until the eggs have set and are light brown underneath, 18 to 20 minutes.

Run a knife around the edge of the pan and invert the tortilla onto a plate. It may be served hot, at room temperature, or cold.

IDIAZABAL AND MIXED PEPPER CROUSTADE

This dish is similar to quiche but uses regional Basque ingredients including peppers, *piment d'Espelette*, and Idiazabal, a sheep's milk cheese named after the town of Idiazabal in the mountainous back country of the Spanish Guipúzcoa province. The cheese is often smoked by the shepherds over green wood fires. Serve the dish warm as an appetizer or a light lunch teamed with a green salad.

SERVES 6 AS AN APPETIZER, 4 OR 5 AS A LUNCH DISH

2 scant cups flour

1½ teaspoons kosher salt

10 tablespoons (1¼ sticks) butter, cubed

¼ cup water, as needed

1 roasted red bell pepper (page 233), peeled and cored

2 roasted green Anaheim chiles

½ pound Idiazabal sheep's milk cheese

1 cup crème fraîche

3 large eggs

Freshly ground white pepper

Pinch of *piment d'Espelette*

On a flat work surface, combine the flour, salt, and butter using your fingers. Rapidly pinch the ingredients together, then let go of them. You want to incorporate the ingredients evenly without warming the butter by handling it too much. You should wind up with a granular—not sticky—consistency. When there are no large chunks of butter remaining, slowly add up to ¼ cup water, kneading it in a little at a time until the dough is evenly mixed and clings together. (It should not be too soft. Depending on the consistency of the dough, you might not have to use all the water.) Form the dough into a flat ball, cover with plastic wrap, and refrigerate for ½ hour.

Preheat the oven to 375 degrees F. and butter the bottom and sides of a 9 × 2-inch tart pan with a removable bottom.

On a lightly floured work surface, roll the dough into a 13-inch circle, approximately ⅛ inch thick. Drape the dough over the rolling pin and transfer it to the prepared tart pan. Unwrap the dough from the pin and press it gently into the pan. Trim the excess pastry by running the rolling pin over the top of the pan.

Line the top and sides of the pastry with parchment paper and gently scatter pie weights or dried beans on top of the paper. Bake until the pastry is partially done, 20 to 25 minutes.

Cut the peppers into ½-inch strips and set aside. Cut the cheese into ½-inch cubes and set aside.

In a large mixing bowl, combine the crème fraîche, eggs, salt to taste, ground white pepper, and *piment d'Espelette*. Mix well and set aside.

As soon as the crust is half baked, remove it from the oven and immediately remove the pie weights and parchment paper. Return the crust to the oven for 2 to 3 minutes, just enough to dry it out slightly.

Remove the crust from the oven again. Scatter the peppers and cheese evenly over the warm crust. Add the egg mixture and return to the oven to bake until firm to the touch and golden brown on top, about 45 minutes. Transfer the croustade to a cooling rack, remove the pan sides, and let it rest for at least 15 minutes.

Serve warm or at room temperature, cut in thick wedges.

PIPÉRADE

Biperrada

SERVES 4 OR 5

½ cup olive oil

8 Anaheim chiles, seeded and finely julienned

1 onion, finely sliced

6 garlic cloves, crushed

6 large vine-ripened tomatoes (about 6 ounces each), peeled and coarsely chopped (about 5 cups)

1 teaspoon sugar

⅛ teaspoon *piment d'Espelette*

1 bay leaf

Kosher salt

½ teaspoon freshly ground white pepper

6 large eggs

Pipérade is a quintessential Basque dish that combines the signature ingredients: tomatoes, onion, garlic, chiles, and controversy. Is it a sauce, side dish, or meal on its own? Should eggs be cooked with the *pipérade*, served alongside, or not used at all? Throughout the Basque country, each version will be slightly different from all the rest. In my family we served eggs and a piece of sautéed ham alongside the *pipérade*. When cooked with eggs, as in this recipe, it may be served as an appetizer, casual luncheon, or light supper dish. Without the eggs, *pipérade* can accompany a range of poultry, meat, or fish.

Warm the olive oil in a large casserole or sauté pan over medium-high heat. Add the chiles, onion, and garlic. Sauté for 5 minutes. Stir in the tomatoes, sugar, *piment d'Espelette*, and bay leaf. Season with salt and pepper to taste and bring to a boil, stirring occasionally. Reduce the heat to a simmer, cover, and cook for 25 to 30 minutes.

Remove and discard the bay leaf. Break the eggs directly into the pan and, using a wooden spoon, stir the ingredients until the eggs are set and all the ingredients have blended. Cook for 5 minutes longer before serving.

Harvesting peppers in the fields near Lodosa.

SOFT-SET EGGS WITH PORCINI MUSHROOMS AND FOIE GRAS

Arraultza Perretxikoak eta Ahate Gibela

This dish is an example of *revuelto* (literally "turned over"), a common method of lightly scrambling eggs with just about any ingredient that comes to hand. It is prepared throughout the Spanish Basque country. I tasted this fabulous combination at the Basque restaurant Elkano in Guetaria, a seacoast town in the Guipúzcoa province. Guetaria was home to Juan Sebastian Elkano, Magellan's only surviving captain. A prominent example of the tenacious Basque character, he completed the round-the-world exploration after Magellan's death, bringing home just one ship and seventeen men of the five ships and hundreds of men who had set out.

SERVES 2 AS A MAIN COURSE OR 4 AS AN APPETIZER

5 large eggs

Kosher salt

Freshly ground white pepper

½ pound foie gras, cut in ¾-inch cubes

1 pound small porcini mushrooms, cut in ¼-inch-thick slices

1 small garlic clove, crushed and finely diced

1 tablespoon chopped fresh parsley

Break the eggs into a bowl, stir lightly with a fork, and set aside.

Sprinkle salt and pepper on the foie gras.

Warm a large sauté pan over high heat. When the pan is very hot, add the foie gras, and sear it until browned, 1 to 1½ minutes. You do not need to add any fat or oil to the pan, as the foie gras will release enough of its own fat when cooking. Remove the foie gras with a slotted spoon and set it aside on paper towels.

Add the mushrooms and garlic to the same pan with the leftover fatty juices from the foie gras, and sauté the mushrooms over medium-high heat until they begin to brown and soften, about 4 minutes. Return the foie gras to the pan, add the eggs, and stir rapidly just until the eggs begin to set, about 45 seconds. Remove from the heat and quickly transfer the mixture to serving plates to prevent the eggs from cooking further. Garnish with parsley, and serve immediately.

ROASTED PIQUILLO PEPPERS WITH FRIED GARLIC VINAIGRETTE

Lodozakoak eta Baratxuri Frijitu Ozpinarekin

This is an extraordinarily simple dish that requires extraordinary ingredients for its flavor. As such it mirrors the essence of Basque cooking. Similar to a red bell pepper, but smaller and more delicate, the *piquillo* pepper is unmatched for its gently spicy flavor and deep red-rosy color. The best *piquillos* are from Lodosa, a town on the Ebro River in the southern tip of Navarra. During the October harvest season, the town and surrounding region are scented with the delicious aroma of roasting peppers. In front of nearly every house you will see women roast the peppers in rotating wire baskets over wood fires. The peppers are frequently served whole as an appetizer as in this recipe or—though it's not traditional—torn into strips and served on top of grilled steak, lamb, or chicken.

SERVES 4

- 2½ tablespoons olive oil
- 12 roasted *piquillo* peppers
- Kosher salt
- Freshly ground white pepper
- 1 garlic clove, very thinly sliced
- 1 tablespoon sherry vinegar
- 2 tablespoons chopped fresh parsley

Preheat the oven to 500 degrees F.

Place 1½ tablespoons olive oil in an ovenproof serving dish large enough to hold the peppers in one layer without overlapping. Season with salt and pepper to taste. Bake until the oil is bubbling hot and the peppers are heated through, 12 to 15 minutes.

Place the remaining 1 tablespoon olive oil in a small sauté pan over high heat. Add the garlic and sauté just until golden. Take care not to burn the garlic, or it will impart a bitter flavor.

Add the sherry vinegar and deglaze by stirring and scraping all over the sides and bottom of the pan to loosen the browned bits.

Remove the peppers from the oven, and pour the garlic sauce on top of them. Sprinkle with parsley and serve immediately.

WILD MUSHROOM RAVIOLI WITH BLACK TRUFFLE

Perretxiko Ravioliak Grisola Beltzekin

This is a luxurious recipe for a dinner party that is more practical than it might look at first glance. The ravioli are made with purchased wonton wrappers and can be prepared ahead. The filling can be used as a stuffing for chicken breasts, a filling for a pastry crust, or a bed for veal scallopini, fish, or even a fillet of beef.

Many Basques support their families by foraging for mushrooms, then selling their loaded baskets at the daily markets where Basque shoppers eagerly snap them up, no matter the price. Truffles, on the other hand, are harder to come by. A few can be found near Campezo, a town in the Alava province. But Basque country is not far from Périgord, home to some of the most aromatic black truffles. Luckily for us in the United States, a wide range of mushrooms, including oyster mushrooms, portobellos, shiitake, and others, are becoming available year round.

SERVES 4

- 5 ounces shiitake mushroom caps (about 4 cups)
- 5 ounces oyster mushroom caps, stems trimmed (about 3¼ cups)
- 5 ounces chanterelle mushrooms (about 2½ cups)
- 2 ounces black trumpet mushrooms (about 2 cups)
- 1½ ounces black truffle
- 7 tablespoons unsalted butter, at room temperature
- 2 shallots, finely diced
- ½ cup dry white wine
- 1½ cups Veal Stock (page 228) or canned low-salt chicken broth
- ¼ cup heavy cream
- Kosher salt
- Freshly ground white pepper
- 1 teaspoon olive oil
- 24 wonton wrappers
- 2 tablespoons snipped fresh chives

Finely dice enough of the shiitake mushroom caps to make about 2½ cups; quarter the remaining shiitake mushrooms and set both aside separately.

Finely dice enough of the oyster mushrooms to make about 2 cups; quarter the remaining oyster mushrooms and set both aside separately.

Finely dice enough of the chanterelle mushrooms to make about 1½ cups; quarter the remaining chanterelle mushrooms and set both aside separately.

Quarter the black trumpet mushrooms and brush away any remaining sand.

Slice two-thirds of the truffle as thinly as possible; finely dice the remaining one-third of the truffle and set both aside separately.

To make the filling, warm 1 tablespoon of the butter in a medium-size sauté pan over medium heat. Add shallots and sauté until translucent, 2 to 3 minutes. Add the finely diced truffle and the finely diced shiitake, oyster, and chanterelle mushrooms and sauté until they are golden brown, about 5 minutes. Add ¼ cup of the white wine and cook until the wine evaporates completely, about 5 more minutes. Add ¼ cup of the veal stock, the cream, and salt and pepper to taste and cook until all of the liquids evaporate completely, about 5 minutes longer. Remove from the heat and immediately spread the filling in a thin layer on a sheet pan; refrigerate until completely cool, about 15 minutes.

Fill a large saucepan half full of water and bring to a boil.

Prepare an ice bath by filling a large bowl with half water and half ice. Add the 1 teaspoon olive oil to the ice bath; set aside.

Line a sheet pan with a damp towel; set aside.

To make the ravioli, lay out 12 wonton wrappers and brush with water. Place 1 tablespoon of filling in the center of each wrapper. Lay a second wrapper on top of each filled one and gently press on the outer edges of the wrappers to seal in the filling, forming the ravioli.

Add 4 to 5 wontons at a time to the boiling water and cook each batch for 1½ minutes. Using a slotted spoon or small strainer, promptly remove the ravioli and transfer them to the ice bath just long enough to stop the cooking process, about 30 seconds. Transfer them to the towel-lined sheet pan. Repeat with the remaining ravioli. The recipe may be made up to this point an hour ahead of time, covered with plastic wrap, and refrigerated. Or wrap very well and freeze the ravioli, even if just for a day, or up to 1 month. Cook them without defrosting, adding 2 to 3 minutes to the cooking time.

Set aside the saucepan of water in which the ravioli were just cooked.

To make the sauce, warm 4 tablespoons of the butter in a medium-size sauté pan over medium-high heat. Add the sliced truffle and all of the quartered shiitake, oyster, chanterelle, and black trumpet mushrooms and sauté for 2 to 3 minutes. Add the

(continued)

remaining ¼ cup white wine and cook until the liquid evaporates completely. Add the remaining 1¼ cups veal stock and bring to a boil. Season with salt and pepper to taste. Add the remaining 2 tablespoons of butter and swirl the ingredients until the butter is completely incorporated.

Return the saucepan of water that the ravioli were first cooked in to a boil. Gently submerge the ravioli in the boiling water just until heated through, about 30 seconds. Carefully lift the ravioli out of the water with a slotted spoon or small strainer.

Arrange 2 to 3 ravioli on each plate, spoon the sauce over the top, and garnish with snipped chives.

TIP: *To store truffles, place them in jar of raw rice and refrigerate. This keeps them fresh longer and the rice becomes permeated with the truffle aroma as well.*

Lorda family homestead, built around 1700.

CORN RISOTTO

Arroza Artoarekin

In Basque country rice is frequently cooked with vegetables or some meat or fish and served as a separate course. But risotto made with the pearly, short-grain Arborio rice has only recently begun to show up on the menus of some of the more adventurous restaurants. Risotto is traditionally served as a first course, but if you love it, make a supper of this dish during corn season.

SERVES 4

6 ears of sweet corn

3 cups water

4 tablespoons unsalted butter

½ cup finely diced onion

2 cups Arborio rice

1 cup dry white wine

2 cups water

¾ cup grated sheep's milk cheese

Kosher salt

Freshly ground white pepper

Using the tip of a sharp knife, slice lengthwise down the center of each row of kernels. Working over a large saucepan, switch to the dull side of a knife, and press down each row of kernels to extract the pulp and juice from the corn, but not the outer kernels. Discard the cobs. Add 3 cups water, and bring to a boil. Simmer for 10 minutes.

Warm 4 tablespoons butter and the onion in a large sauté pan over high heat; sauté until translucent but not browned, 2 to 3 minutes. Stir in the Arborio rice, coating it evenly with the butter and onion. Reduce the heat slightly, and add the white wine while stirring constantly with a wooden spoon. When the liquid is gone, add 1 cup of the simmering water the corn was cooked in, and continue stirring the rice until the liquid evaporates. Repeat until all the corn-water has been incorporated, 1 cup at a time, followed by 2 cups of water if necessary. Begin tasting the rice for doneness after 15 to 20 minutes. Cook until the risotto is moist, creamy, and al dente. It is done when the rice appears opaque, not bright white, in about 25 minutes.

Stir in the cheese and season with salt and pepper to taste. Serve immediately.

TIP: *Preparing the corn in this fashion extracts all the flavor and leaves the tough kernel skins still attached to the cob.*

EGGPLANT AND GOAT CHEESE ROLLS WITH TOMATO SALAD

Goat cheese is rare in the Basque country, so I was quite excited when I spotted some handmade cheeses at the Wednesday market in Ordizia in the Spanish province of Guipúzcoa. The market was first established by a decree of King Alfonso the Wise in 1268 and has been held continuously since 1798. The whole town buzzes on market day, and the prices at Ordizia set the prices for all the surrounding markets. Vendors arrange their vibrant displays under the stone-pillared roof, piling the colorful produce in big baskets or arranging pyramids of cheeses on folding tables draped in red-and-white checked fabric. While not typically Basque, all the ingredients for this dish would be found at Ordizia's summer market. The tomato salad tastes great on its own or served as a side dish for fish, cold chicken, or sliced lamb.

SERVES 4

- 4 medium-size eggplants (about 1 pound each)
- Kosher salt
- 3 tablespoons plus 1 teaspoon olive oil
- Freshly ground white pepper
- 5½ ounces fresh goat cheese, softened and separated into 12 equal pieces
- 4 large vine-ripened tomatoes (about 1½ pounds), peeled and cored
- 3 tablespoons extra-virgin olive oil
- 2 tablespoons snipped fresh chives
- 2 tablespoons julienned fresh basil
- 1 tablespoon chopped fresh parsley
- 1 teaspoon crushed coriander seeds

Preheat the oven to 400 degrees F.

Slice 3 eggplants in half and incise the meat in diagonally intersecting lines, approximately 1 inch apart and ½ inch deep. Sprinkle liberally with salt and set aside for at least 20 minutes. Wipe off the salt and place the eggplant halves on a sheet pan, skin side down. Brush the meat with 3 tablespoons olive oil. Cover with aluminum foil and bake until soft throughout, about 40 minutes. When done, remove the eggplants from the oven and set aside to cool completely.

Using a mandoline or sharp knife, cut the remaining whole eggplant into 12 very thin lengthwise slices. Sprinkle with salt and set aside for 15 minutes.

When the baked eggplant is cool, remove all of the soft pulpy meat and discard the skin. Finely chop the eggplant meat and place it in a mixing bowl with salt and pepper to taste.

Line a sheet pan with parchment paper and brush with the remaining 1 teaspoon of olive oil; set aside.

Pat the uncooked eggplant slices dry, then place 1 tablespoon of the eggplant meat and 1 piece of goat cheese in the middle of each slice. Roll them up and place them flap side down on the prepared sheet pan. Bake until cooked through, about 20 minutes. Remove from the oven, and set aside to cool, about 30 minutes.

To make the tomato and herb salad, cut the tomatoes in half and squeeze gently to remove the seeds. Coarsely dice the tomato and place it in a large bowl with the extra-virgin olive oil, chives, basil, parsley, coriander seeds, and salt and pepper to taste; toss well.

Place the tomato salad in the center of a serving platter or on individual plates. Lay the baked eggplant rolls on top. Brush or spritz them lightly with olive oil.

TIP: *To crush coriander, use a mortar and pestle or place the seeds in a heavy plastic bag or in a clean tea towel and press down hard with the bottom of a heavy pan or rubber mallet.*

VARIATION: *If you want to be really easy on yourself, the cooked eggplant can be used on its own as a tasty sandwich filling with chunks of goat cheese and a few leaves of basil.*

Cheese vendor at Ordizia.

RAGOUT OF ROASTED VEGETABLES

Vegetable stews are found throughout Spain as well as in Basque terrain. One example is *pisto,* which must include potatoes. Another is *menestra,* which routinely includes a bit of meat. Of course these vegetable stews have a festival devoted to them. Olite, a small town in the middle of the fertile fields of southern Navarra, celebrates *menestra* each April when the spring vegetables appear. These ragouts commonly include asparagus, baby artichokes, peas, and fava beans, but the ingredients change with the seasons. They are not stews as we might think of them. Instead, the vegetables are roasted in olive oil and butter, creating a dish full of deep flavors. It is delicious as an appetizer but is so good you may want to make supper out of it by serving it with crusty bread and a wedge of sheep's milk cheese.

SERVES 4

¼ cup olive oil

6 tablespoons (¾ stick) unsalted butter

4 garlic cloves

4 medium cipollini onions, peeled

8 baby carrots

4 cleaned artichoke bottoms, cut in half

3 medium parsnips (about ½ pound), cored and cut in a thick julienne

3 stalks salsify (about ½ pound), peeled and cut into 3-inch-long pieces

6 small Yukon Gold potatoes (about 8 ounces), halved

1 tablespoon chopped fresh thyme

2 teaspoons kosher salt

¼ teaspoon freshly ground white pepper

16 asparagus spears, trimmed and cut into 3-inch pieces

1 tablespoon chopped fresh parsley

Preheat the oven to 500 degrees F.

Warm the olive oil, butter, and garlic in a large casserole over medium-high heat. Add the cipollini onions, baby carrots, and artichoke bottoms and sauté for 2 to 3 minutes. Add the parsnips, salsify, potatoes, thyme, salt, and pepper. Stir the vegetables using a wooden spoon, cover, and put in the oven for 10 minutes.

Gently stir the vegetables, then add the asparagus and continue to cook until all of the vegetables are soft and tender, 10 to 12 minutes longer. Garnish with parsley.

TIP: *Salsify and artichokes discolor soon after being cut. To prevent this, squeeze the juice of 1 or 2 lemons into a bowl of cold water and add the vegetables to it as soon as you have finished preparing them for cooking.*

PIQUILLO PEPPER, ROSEMARY, AND WHITE BEAN GRATIN

I particularly like gratins. They are easily assembled, require little attention while cooking, and because of their crusty tops, have wonderful, contrasting textures. The oven baking brings out deep, sweet flavors not easily achieved on top of the stove. When I was asked to contribute a recipe that would help the organization "Food and Wines from Spain" familiarize American chefs with Spanish ingredients, I developed this, to accent the delicious wood-roasted peppers from Lodosa. It is a warm and comforting appetizer or supper dish for a chilly winter's day.

SERVES 6 AS AN APPETIZER, 4 AS A SUPPER DISH

4 cups cooked small white northern beans

2 tablespoons extra-virgin olive oil

1 teaspoon chopped fresh rosemary

1 teaspoon kosher salt

¼ teaspoon freshly ground white pepper

4 tablespoons (½ stick) unsalted butter, melted

¼ cup Vegetable Stock (page 229)

One 13-ounce can roasted *piquillo* peppers

3 to 4 ounces semisoft sheep's milk cheese, thinly shaved

1½ tablespoons toasted bread crumbs

1 tablespoon chopped fresh parsley

Preheat the oven to 475 degrees F.

Using a food mill or processor, puree the cooked beans, and transfer them to a large mixing bowl. Add the extra-virgin olive oil and combine well. Stir in the rosemary, salt, and pepper. Add the melted butter and vegetable stock and mix well.

Smooth one third of the bean puree on the bottom of an ovenproof serving dish. Cover the layer of puree entirely with a layer of *piquillo* peppers. Repeat this step for the second layer. Finish with the remaining one third of the bean puree on top.

Spread the shaved cheese evenly over the bean puree. Sprinkle the toasted bread crumbs and white pepper to taste on top, and place the dish in the oven until the surface is lightly browned and slightly crusty on top, about 15 minutes.

Remove from the oven, garnish with chopped parsley, and serve immediately.

BAYONNE HAM AND SHEEP'S MILK CHEESE TERRINE

Urdai Azpikoa eta Ardi Gasna Kaxolan

This recipe combines two of the choicest ingredients of Basque cuisine: Bayonne ham and sheep's milk cheese. It is very easy to put together, especially if you ask your butcher to slice the ham and cheese. Sautéed and served on lightly dressed greens as described here, it makes an elegant first course or luncheon dish. Or the terrine can simply be sliced and served at room temperature as a make-ahead buffet dish.

TERRINE SERVES 8 TO 10, SALAD SERVES 4

TERRINE

1½ pounds Bayonne ham, sliced ⅛ inch thick

1½ pounds sheep's milk cheese, sliced ⅛ inch thick

VINAIGRETTE

½ teaspoon sherry vinegar

1½ teaspoons extra-virgin olive oil

½ tablespoon chopped fresh parsley

Kosher salt

Freshly ground white pepper

4 handfuls frisée lettuce or other salad greens

1 teaspoon olive oil

All-purpose flour

Pinch of *piment d'Espelette*

Cut the ham and the cheese into 20 to 23 very thin slices each, with a minimum measurement of 9½ × 3½ inches. It is better to have slightly larger slices that can be trimmed to fit the terrine exactly than to have pieces that are too small.

Line a 9½ × 3½ × 3½-inch terrine generously with plastic wrap, leaving enough overhang to cover the top of the terrine when it is filled.

Starting with a layer of cheese, alternate layers of ham and cheese until the mold is completely filled, approximately twenty layers of each. Cover the top with the overlapping plastic wrap and press down firmly. Refrigerate overnight.

Unmold by firmly pulling the plastic up and out of the mold. Place on a cutting board, and using a very sharp knife, cut as many ½-inch-thick slices as you will be serving and store the remaining terrine in the refrigerator for up to 1 week.

To make the vinaigrette, stir together all of the ingredients in a small bowl.

Arrange the frisée on each of four plates, dress the lettuce with the vinaigrette, and set aside.

Warm the olive oil in a nonstick pan over high heat.

Lightly dust both sides of the terrine slices with flour and add them to the pan. Working very quickly, sauté the slices on both sides just until lightly browned, but not long enough to melt the cheese, approximately 30 to 60 seconds. Lay 1 slice on top of each salad, sprinkle with *piment d'Espelette,* and serve immediately.

COUNTRY-STYLE PÂTÉ

When I asked my mother for her pâté recipe, she laughed and reminded me how squeamish I used to be during pig butchering season. It seemed to me then that the streets were full of the sound of pigs' squeals. I could never bring myself to help dismantle a pig, but I did help in the kitchen when it was time to make the blood sausage, ham, confit, pâté, rillettes, and andouille. At noon, there would be a big, boisterous lunch; then everyone would return to work on the pig. By the end of the weekend, all who helped went home loaded down with the delicious proceeds of their efforts.

TERRINE SERVES 10 TO 12

1 pound skinned pork jowl, finely diced (see Tip)

1 pound pork liver, diced in 1-inch cubes

Caul fat

½ cup dry white wine

1 tablespoon brandy

½ tablespoon sugar

½ teaspoon *quatre-épices* (a mixture of equal parts ground nutmeg, white pepper, cloves, and ginger; it can be homemade or store-bought)

½ teaspoon *piment d'Espelette*

½ tablespoon kosher salt

¼ tablespoon juniper berries

2 small eggs

2 small garlic cloves, crushed

3 bay leaves

Run the pork jowl and liver through a meat grinder with a medium-size ring, or chop it until it is coarsely pureed.

Line a 9½ × 3½ × 3½-inch terrine, or small loaf pan, with enough caul fat to overlap the top of the terrine; set aside.

In a large mixing bowl, combine the meat, wine, brandy, sugar, *quatre-épices*, *piment d'Espelette*, salt, juniper berries, eggs, and garlic; mix well. Fill the terrine with the pâté and place the bay leaves on top. Fold the overlapping caul fat over the pâté. Cover with a lid or plastic wrap, and refrigerate for 24 hours.

Preheat the oven to 375 degrees F.

Stand the terrine in a large roasting pan filled with a few inches of hot water and cook until a fork, when inserted, comes out clean, about 1½ hours. Set aside to cool. Refrigerate, covered, for up to 1 week. Serve cold or at room temperature. Remove bay leaves before serving.

TIP: *Even in Europe, for anyone not butchering his own pig, it is necessary to call the butcher and order the pork jowl meat ahead of time. Pork jowl is an ideal cut for pâté because its high proportion of fat means that no more needs to be added to the recipe.*

SAUTÉED FOIE GRAS WITH GRAPES AND VERJUS

Ahate Gibela Sukardun Mahatsekin

Foie gras is available throughout the French Basque provinces thanks to the influence of neighboring Gascony. It is eaten both fresh and preserved. Once a year my family would can foie gras. The jars were then opened only for special occasions. Now when I go home, the first thing my mother says is, "Let's open a little jar of foie gras for us tonight." I particularly love it prepared warm as in this recipe. A quick pass in a hot sauté pan thoroughly sears the outside and gives the foie gras a thin, crispy exterior and a buttery, melting interior. The grapes and *verjus* (the juice from unripe grapes) add a gentle acidity that balances the overall effect of the dish.

SERVES 4

- 4 diagonally cut slices fresh foie gras (about 3 ounces each)
- Kosher salt
- Freshly ground white pepper
- 4 pinches of sugar
- 1 cup halved seedless grapes
- ⅓ cup *verjus* (page 21)
- ¼ cup Veal Stock (page 228)
- 6 tablespoons (¾ stick) unsalted butter, softened
- 1 small head of frisée lettuce

Sprinkle both sides of each slice of foie gras with salt, pepper, and a pinch of sugar.

Place a large sauté pan over high heat. When the pan is really hot, add the foie gras and sear for about 45 seconds on each side. You do not need to add any fat or oil to the pan, as the foie gras will release enough of its own fat when cooking. With a slotted spoon, transfer the foie gras to paper towels.

Discard the fatty juices from the pan before returning it to high heat. Add the grapes and *verjus* and deglaze the pan by stirring and scraping all over the sides and bottom of the pan to loosen the browned bits. Bring to a boil. Add the veal stock and return to a boil. Swirl in the butter. Season with salt and pepper to taste.

Return the seared foie gras to the pan just until warmed through, 30 to 45 seconds.

To serve, evenly distribute the frisée lettuce among four plates. Lay a slice of foie gras on top of the frisée, and spoon the grapes and sauce evenly over the top.

TIP: *Obtain the proper grade for the type of dish you are preparing. "A" grade is top quality and what you want for a dish like this, where very little is done to the foie gras and you eat it immediately. "B" is slightly inferior and would be well suited for simple terrines or dishes where there are a number of other ingredients competing for attention. "C" is best for sauces where you want the flavor and richness, but the texture is not important.*

CALAMARI À LA GOULUE

Txipiroi Goulueren Moduan

On a visit to Biarritz in 1997, I had an outstanding calamari dish prepared in this simple style in the restaurant La Goulue. When I asked the chef what he did to the calamari, he replied, "Very little. What makes them so good is that they were line caught at six A.M. and here you are eating them at noon." My lunch was a forceful demonstration of the best of Basque cooking: exquisite ingredients simply prepared.

SERVES 4

2 pounds cleaned squid, without tentacles

3 tablespoons olive oil

1 teaspoon minced garlic

5 tablespoons chopped fresh parsley

2 pinches of *piment d'Espelette*

Kosher salt

Freshly ground white pepper

1 wedge of fresh lemon

Preheat oven to 275 degrees F.

Slice the squid crosswise into rings as thinly as possible, preferably less than ⅛ inch thick. Rinse in a bowl of cold water, drain, and pat very dry. Set aside.

Warm a medium-large ovenproof serving dish in the oven on low heat.

Warm half of the olive oil in a medium sauté pan over high heat. When the oil is really hot but not smoking, add half of the garlic and half of the squid rings. Sauté for 30 seconds. Add half of the parsley, a pinch of *piment d'Espelette,* and salt and pepper to taste. Sauté for another 30 seconds, or just until cooked through but still tender. Transfer to the warmed serving dish in the oven. Repeat with the remaining oil, garlic, squid, parsley, and *piment d'Espelette,* and season with salt and pepper. Add to the serving dish. Squeeze the lemon on top and serve immediately.

Harbor of St.-Jean-de-Luz.

ELVERS

Angulak

This is a traditional Basque recipe for elvers, an eagerly awaited seasonal delicacy. Elvers or baby eels are known as *piballes* in French and *angulas* in Spanish. The adult eels swim to the Sargasso Sea to spawn. Unbelievably, it takes the young eels 3 years to follow their instincts back to the waters of their parents. There they are caught by the thousands, cleaned, prepared for cooking, and sold in markets for prices as high as $200 a pound. It is a testament to the high priority Basques place on their stomachs and their traditional dishes that price is no hindrance. The spaghetti-slim, 4-inch-long eels are cooked with olive oil, garlic, and red pepper, consumed with gusto, and then talked and argued about as they have been for centuries. Did the elvers have black backs? These are considered to have the finest flavor. Were they as plentiful as last year? Are the elvers from the mouth of the Adour superior to the ones from the mouth of the Nivelle? Only another helping will settle the argument. Or maybe it won't . . . Fresh elvers may not be available in the United States; however, frozen elvers are (see page 245 for a listing).

SERVES 4

⅓ cup sherry vinegar

6 cups water

3 tablespoons olive oil

2 garlic cloves, thinly sliced

1 small dried red chile pepper, halved and seeded

½ pound elvers

Kosher salt

Freshly ground white pepper

Combine the sherry vinegar and water in a large saucepan and bring to a boil.

Blend the olive oil, garlic, and chile pepper in a 6½-inch *cazuela* or heavy-bottomed saucepan and set aside.

Plunge the elvers into the boiling vinegar water for 30 seconds. Strain and set aside.

Quickly place the *cazuela* with the oil, garlic, and chile over high heat. As soon as the garlic begins to brown, add the eels. Sauté them over high heat for about 1 minute, stirring them around in the oil with a wooden spoon. Season with salt and pepper to taste and serve immediately.

JUMBO PRAWNS À LA PLANCHA

Izkirak a la Plantxa

Known as *gambas à la plancha* in Spain, this casual manner of preparing prawns has been adopted throughout the Basque region. It is an ideal food for parties and for those who love to eat. Since the prawns are served whole, to eat them you must use your fingers. Everyone gets a little messy, and that creates a relaxed atmosphere. The prawns can be sautéed or grilled with equal success.

SERVES 4

20 whole jumbo prawns, preferably with heads on (about 1½ pounds)

3 tablespoons sherry vinegar

4 garlic cloves, finely sliced

¼ cup olive oil

2 teaspoons dried chile flakes

Pinch of kosher salt

1 lemon, thinly sliced crosswise

Spread the prawns out in one layer in a large *cazuela* or ovenproof glass baking dish.

Combine the sherry vinegar, garlic, olive oil, chile flakes, and salt. Mix well and pour over the prawns. Turn them over a few times in the marinade to coat well. Scatter the lemon slices on top. Cover with plastic wrap and refrigerate for 2 to 3 hours.

Remove from the refrigerator a half hour before cooking and drain the prawns, reserving the marinade.

Preheat a griddle or large sauté pan to medium-high.

Place half of the prawns on the hot griddle and drizzle half of the marinade on top. Cook for 3 to 4 minutes, turning them once or twice, until cooked through. Repeat with the remaining prawns and marinade. Serve immediately.

MARINATED ANCHOVIES

When I think of anchovies, I immediately picture the proud old woman who sells the lustrous little fish on a weather-worn table on the perimeter of the La Brecha market in San Sebastián. Come rain or shine, you will find her carefully cleaning the anchovies and then tenderly wrapping them in cabbage leaves and again in newsprint. To me there are only two ways to eat anchovies: either *à la plancha* (cooked on a griddle) with olive oil, garlic, and fresh rosemary), or marinated. Marinated anchovies, like those in this recipe, are a staple of San Sebastián's *pintxos* bars. I love to serve them with a little chopped egg or a tomato salad, or on crunchy toast with a sprinkling of *fleur de sel* (gray salt hand-harvested from salt ponds on France's Atlantic shore).

SERVES 4 TO 6

1 pound fresh anchovies
3 tablespoons fresh lemon juice
3 tablespoons sherry vinegar
1 teaspoon kosher salt
Freshly ground white pepper
⅓ cup cold water
Olive oil to garnish

Tear the heads off the anchovies and run your fingers along the spine to remove all the innards. Pull out the bone.

Rinse the fillets under cold running water, spread them out on a towel, and pat dry. Lay the anchovies in a single layer in a shallow nonreactive platter.

Combine the lemon juice, sherry vinegar, salt, pepper, and water and pour over the anchovies. Cover with plastic wrap and set aside in the refrigerator to marinate for 2 hours.

Drain the marinade, and drizzle olive oil to taste over the anchovies. Serve them in salads, with roasted peppers or hard-boiled eggs, or on small toasts.

SARDINES

Santurce, a small town in the suburbs of Bilbao in Vizcaya province, is famous for its sardines. A local folk song recalls the days when the young, long-legged wives of fishermen delivered the day's catch on the run, carrying baskets of fresh fish on their heads. Loosely translated, here is the first verse:

From Santurce to Bilbao
I run along the shore   *And shout in the street,*
With my skirts held up   *Who wants to buy fresh sardines?*
To show off my legs.   *My little sardines are delicious.*
I run very fast   *I am from Santurce*
Despite my corset   *And I will bring them to you!*

When sardines are at their best, in the summer months and fresh off the boat, they are cooked *à la plancha* (on a griddle) and often become the centerpiece of a spontaneous feast. Sautéeing fresh sardines makes the most of their exquisite, rich flavor. Splash them with a little sherry vinegar or lemon juice just before serving.

SERVES 4 TO 6

2 pounds (about 12) fresh sardines, gutted and cleaned

Kosher salt

Freshly ground white pepper

1 cup flour

2 to 4 tablespoons olive oil

Sherry vinegar or freshly squeezed lemon juice

Rinse the sardines under clear running water. Pat them dry with paper towels to remove any scales; set aside.

Sprinkle the sardines with salt and pepper, dredge them in flour, and set aside.

Warm 2 tablespoons olive oil in a large nonstick sauté pan over high heat.

Place 4 to 6 sardines in the pan at a time and sauté for 2½ minutes on each side. Transfer to a serving platter.

If necessary, warm 2 more tablespoons olive oil in the same pan; otherwise, just repeat step 4.

Just before serving, drizzle with sherry vinegar or lemon juice to taste.

TUNA CONFIT

The inspiration for this dish comes from the classic method for preserving tuna during its peak season, when families all along the coast can their own. This flavorful tuna turns picnics into feasts. Try it flaked over a Niçoise salad; or served with Onion Marmalade (page 102), Roasted Peppers (page 233), and fresh bread; or tossed with a tomato salad or hard-boiled eggs.

SERVES 4 TO 6

1½ pounds albacore tuna fillet

1 tablespoon kosher salt

2 bay leaves

3 cups olive oil, or more if needed

8 garlic cloves

1 tablespoon black peppercorns

2 cloves

1 mild dried chile

Sprinkle both sides of the tuna fillet with salt. Lay the bay leaves on the fillet, cover with plastic wrap, and set aside for 1 hour.

Place the tuna and the bay leaves in a large, deep saucepan. Add the olive oil (3 cups should be enough to cover the tuna, but if not, add extra oil to make sure the fillet is covered).

Add the garlic, peppercorns, cloves, and dried chile, and bring to a boil.

Reduce the heat to a slow simmer and cook for 1 hour.

Using a slotted spoon, remove the tuna, and set aside to cool.

Strain the olive oil through a fine-mesh sieve and discard the garlic, bay leaves, and spices. Reserve the olive oil to use as a dressing for salads or as a dipping sauce for bread. Use the tuna within 2 days.

TUNA TARTARE

Tuna tartare was rarely seen in the Basque country until this last decade, when it suddenly became fashionable. This recipe requires very little time or attention but does require very fresh fish cut from the heart of the fillet. Serve with a green salad, lots of toasted country bread, and a glass of chilled rosé wine.

SERVES 4 TO 6

1 pound ahi tuna fillet, very finely diced

2 tablespoons finely diced shallots

2 tablespoons snipped fresh chives

2 tablespoons mayonnaise

1 tablespoon extra-virgin olive oil

½ teaspoon kosher salt

¼ teaspoon freshly ground white pepper

¼ teaspoon *piment d'Espelette*

1 tablespoon capers

1 tablespoon freshly squeezed lemon juice

Mix all of the ingredients together until incorporated. Refrigerate for a half hour before serving.

La Brecha seafood market in San Sebastián.

HARICOTS VERTS SALAD WITH FIGS AND WALNUT VINAIGRETTE

Leka eta Pikuen Entsalada Intxaur Olio-Ozpinetan

Haricots verts are very popular in Basque cooking. Even though my mother did not have a *potager*, when these slim green beans were in season, she would buy enough of them to can for the winter months. In the United States' markets the beans are called haricots verts or French green beans. Their season overlaps with that of figs, another of my favorite summer foods. Additionally, with so many walnut trees growing here in Northern California as they do in the yards of many Basque *caserios* (farmhouses), I've added both whole walnuts and walnut oil to the salad. Basque cooks love to use these toasty nuts in salads and meat dishes such as Lamb Stew with Mixed Nut Pesto (page 140), as well as in such rustic desserts as Walnut Cream (page 213) and Walnut and Sheep's Milk Cheese Gratin (page 216).

SERVES 4 AS AN APPETIZER

- 1 pound haricots verts (slim green beans), tipped and tailed
- Kosher salt
- 2 tablespoons sherry vinegar
- ⅛ teaspoon freshly ground white pepper
- 3 tablespoons toasted walnut oil
- 1 tablespoon olive oil
- 2 tablespoons snipped fresh chives
- 2 tablespoons finely chopped fresh parsley
- 1 tablespoon very finely diced shallot
- 6 large ripe figs, stemmed and quartered
- 20 small basil leaves
- 2 tablespoons coarsely chopped walnuts
- ¼ ounce summer truffle, very thinly sliced (optional; see Tip)

Bring a large pot of water to a boil and add a large pinch of salt. Prepare a large ice water bath; set aside.

Drop the beans into the boiling water, and cook at a full boil until they are slightly tender and cooked through, about 6 to 8 minutes. Drain, plunge into the ice water to halt the cooking process, drain again, and spread the beans on a kitchen towel.

Combine the sherry vinegar, ⅛ teaspoon kosher salt, pepper, walnut oil, and olive oil in a large mixing bowl. Whisk vigorously. Add the chives, parsley, and shallot and mix well. Drop the figs, beans, basil leaves, and walnuts into the bowl, and toss together gently but thoroughly with your hands. Sprinkle the salad with a pinch of salt and, if desired, garnish with thinly sliced summer truffle. Serve immediately.

TIP: *The best way to cook haricots verts to retain their color is in an unlined copper pot. I use the round bowl I have for beating egg whites and simply balance it on the stove's burner. A reaction takes place that helps the beans retain their green color. Do cook the beans sufficiently. They should be tender and just slightly resistant when done. And remember to dress your salad only just before serving. If the salad sits and waits, the acid in the dressing will turn the beans army green.*

MARINATED TOMATO, ONION, AND PEPPER SALAD

In the summer our family meals would often begin with a tomato salad such as this one. The primary ingredients—tomatoes, onion, and *piments de pays*—represent the Basque flavor triumvirate (as well as the colors of the Basque flag), ingredients joined together over and over again in endless variations, the most famous of which is probably *Pipérade* (page 46). Try this dish on a very hot day when its temperature, as well as its flavors, will be sure to pique flagging appetites.

SERVES 4 TO 6

6 vine-ripened tomatoes (about 6 ounces each), peeled and cored

¼ small red onion, very thinly sliced

½ Anaheim chile, seeded and finely julienned

4 tablespoons extra-virgin olive oil

2 tablespoons balsamic vinegar

1 teaspoon kosher salt

Freshly ground white pepper

Slice the tomatoes as thinly as possible. In a shallow serving platter, fan the tomatoes in long rows.

Scatter the onion and pepper on top of the tomatoes and drizzle the oil and vinegar over the salad. Cover tightly with plastic wrap, and refrigerate for 3 hours or even overnight.

Just before serving, sprinkle the salad with salt and pepper to taste.

Overlooking Ascarat.

WHITE ASPARAGUS SALAD

Zainzuri Txuri Entsalada

Growing up, I thought asparagus was always white. It is the preferred asparagus throughout Spain and the Basque country and is served as an appetizer or in the classic Hake San Sebastián Style (page 90). Much as I love white asparagus, green asparagus is equally (and maybe even more) delicious, so feel free to make this simple salad with any variety, even the purple asparagus if you come across it at your farmers' market.

SERVES 4

2 quarts water

Juice of 1 small lemon

3½ teaspoons kosher salt

32 white asparagus spears

String

1 tablespoon Dijon mustard

1 tablespoon sherry vinegar

¼ cup extra-virgin olive oil

2 tablespoons chopped fresh parsley

2 tablespoons chopped fresh shallots

2 tablespoons snipped chives

Prepare a "holding bowl" with 2 quarts of water and the fresh lemon juice; set aside.

Fill a large saucepan three-quarters full of water. Bring to a boil and add 3 teaspoons salt.

Carefully peel and trim the asparagus into evenly sized spears, about 4 inches long and ½ inch wide. After trimming each spear, place it in the holding bowl to prevent it from discoloring.

Arrange the spears in 4 even bundles, and gently tie each bundle with string at the top and bottom. This helps to keep the delicate spears from bruising while cooking.

Add the bundles to the boiling water, and cook until the asparagus is tender, 12 to 15 minutes.

Combine the mustard, remaining ½ teaspoon salt, sherry vinegar, and extra-virgin olive oil in a small bowl, and stir together well. Add the parsley, shallots, and chives. Stir, then set aside.

Snip open the bundles of asparagus, discard the string, and lay 1 bundle on each plate, with all of the spears facing in the same direction and placed closely together. Spoon the sauce in a thick band across the center of the asparagus.

ROASTED POTATO SALAD WITH LEMON ZEST AND FRESH HERBS

SERVES 4

4 medium lemons

20 small Yukon Gold or white creamer potatoes (about 1¾ pounds), cut in half

3 tablespoons olive oil

3 large sprigs chopped fresh thyme

¾ tablespoon plus ½ teaspoon kosher salt

Freshly ground black pepper

1 quart vegetable oil (see Tip)

Flour for dredging

1 tablespoon freshly squeezed lemon juice or more to taste

4 tablespoons extra-virgin olive oil

1 tablespoon snipped fresh chives

Lemons grow in the Mediterranean climate of southern Navarra, protected by mountains from the wind and storms of the Atlantic. Yet most Basque cooks consider lemons nothing more than a garnish for fish. I've used lemons in three ways for this dish. First, half of the zest is roasted with the potatoes, taking on a complex sweet-sour taste from the oven roasting. The remaining zest is blanched and then deep-fried, which adds both crunch and sweetness. Finally, the lemon juice is used in the vinaigrette for this appetizing salad or side dish.

Preheat the oven to 425 degrees F.

Line a sheet pan with parchment paper, brush with olive oil, and set aside.

Cut the top and bottoms off the lemons so they will stand upright on a cutting surface. Using a knife or swivel-bladed vegetable peeler, peel the lemons in thick strips, from top to bottom, including as little white pith as possible. Cut half of the peel lengthwise into a fine julienne and set aside.

In a large mixing bowl, combine the potatoes, olive oil, thick lemon peel strips, thyme, ¾ tablespoon salt, and pepper to taste. Toss well and place the potatoes cut side down on the prepared sheet pan. Pour any remaining oil, herbs, and peel from the bowl over the potatoes.

Roast until the potatoes are cooked through and tender, about 25 minutes.

Heat the vegetable oil in a deep fryer or heavy-bottomed saucepan to approximately 375 degrees F.

Blanch the finely julienned lemon peel by placing it in a saucepan with cold water to cover and bringing to a boil. Remove from the heat, strain, and rinse immediately under cold water. Repeat the process. Blot dry with paper towels.

Dredge the blanched lemon peel in flour, shaking off any excess. Fry just until golden brown, 45 seconds to 1 minute. Remove it, using a slotted spoon, and scatter it on a paper towel.

To make the vinaigrette, whisk the lemon juice, extra-virgin olive oil, remaining ½ teaspoon salt, and pepper to taste in a small bowl until well combined.

Arrange 9 to 10 potato halves in the center of each plate. Spoon equal amounts of vinaigrette on the potatoes, and top with a tall pile of fried lemon zest. Garnish each plate with chives and a few turns of freshly ground black pepper.

TIP: *While frying the peel may seem a bit of work, the results are worth it. Let the frying oil cool, then filter it back into the bottle to reuse. For instance, fish fried in the lemon-scented oil would taste wonderful.*

FISH AND SHELLFISH

FISH

CUTTLEFISH STEAK WITH
ALMOND AND LEMON BUTTER
78

STUFFED SQUID IN INK SAUCE
80

FISH CAKE JUAN MARI   82

WARM CODFISH AND
POTATO SALAD   84

HALIBUT CHEEKS WITH GARLIC
AND PARSLEY   85

PEPPERS STUFFED WITH
SALT COD   86

SALT COD "AL PIL-PIL"   88

FRESH CODFISH WITH
BASQUAISE SAUCE   89

HAKE SAN SEBASTIÁN STYLE
90

SEA BREAM WITH GARLIC
VINAIGRETTE "À LA CONCHA"
93

SOLE BRAISED WITH
CÈPES AND TXACOLI   94

POACHED TROUT WITH TOMATO
VINAIGRETTE   96

HALIBUT BRAISED WITH
CLAMS IN GREEN PEA SALSA
98

MONKFISH IN RED WINE WITH
LEEKS AND PANCETTA   99

BAKED SALMON FILLET WITH
RED PEPPER SABAYON   100

SEARED AHI TUNA STEAKS
WITH ONION MARMALADE
102

YELLOWFIN TUNA AND
POTATO STEW   104

WHOLE ROASTED SEA BASS
105

SHELLFISH

CHERRYSTONE CLAMS WITH
GARLIC AND PARSLEY   106

STEAMED MUSSELS WITH
TOMATO   107

SEA SCALLOP SAUTÉ WITH
ARTICHOKES AND ROASTED
PEPPERS   108

CRAB AND POTATO GRATIN
109

SAUTÉED PRAWNS IN PASTIS
WITH LEMON AND CHERRY
TOMATOES   110

SEAFOOD AND SHELLFISH
STEW   112

CUTTLEFISH STEAK WITH ALMOND AND LEMON BUTTER

SERVES 4

½ cup sliced blanched almonds

4 large cuttlefish (about 6 ounces each), cleaned

About ¾ cup olive oil

4 garlic cloves, thinly sliced

¾ teaspoon coriander seeds, crushed

1 tablespoon chopped fresh rosemary

1 tablespoon black peppercorns

½ teaspoon kosher salt

Freshly ground white pepper

6 tablespoons (¾ stick) unsalted butter

3 tablespoons freshly squeezed lemon juice

Cuttlefish are related to squid and octopus, but their ink is a reddish-brown (it is used in sepia-colored paint). They are cooked in the same way as squid and are especially popular in the Guipúzcoa province, where they are frequently cut into "steaks" and cooked on a hot griddle. The flesh does need to be pounded, like abalone, to be tender. It should be cooked for either a long time or very quickly as in this recipe. Use a foil-wrapped brick or another weight on top of the "steaks" to keep them from curling. Serve with a pile of Fried Garlic Potatoes (page 168) or Creamy Mashed Potatoes (page 169).

Sauté the almonds in a nonstick pan over medium-high heat until lightly toasted, about 2 minutes. Set aside.

Split all of the cuttlefish open so that they lie flat. Place them on a cutting board or flat surface with their exterior side facing up. Lightly incise the flesh in a crisscross pattern every ½ inch. Pat dry and place the steaks in a shallow glass baking dish.

Add ½ cup olive oil, garlic, coriander seeds, rosemary, peppercorns, and ½ teaspoon salt. Cover with plastic wrap and set aside in a refrigerator for 4 to 6 hours.

Remove the cuttlefish from the marinade, pat dry, and sprinkle both sides with salt and pepper to taste.

Warm 1 tablespoon olive oil on a griddle or in a sauté pan over high heat.

Cook 1 steak at a time, incised side down first, and top with a weight. (This is important; otherwise your cuttlefish will curl). Sauté until golden brown and cooked through, 1½ to 2 minutes on each side.

Repeat with each steak, adding a few teaspoons of olive oil to the pan before cooking each additional steak.

Either in the same pan in which the steaks were cooked, or in a separate pan if you've used a griddle, cook the butter on medium-high heat until lightly browned. Add the lemon juice, toasted almonds, and salt and pepper to taste. Swirl the sauce in the pan, then spoon it over the steaks. Serve immediately.

Remelluri winery in the Rioja Alavesa.

STUFFED SQUID IN INK SAUCE

Txipiroia Beren Saltsan

To my dismay, people often refuse to try this absolutely delicious dish because of its color. Black. Yet squid stuffed with this savory mix of garlic, onion, and bacon, slowly cooked in a rich sauce until nearly fork-tender, is one of the most tantalizing dishes of the Guipúzcoa region. Though everyone claims to have his or her secret way to prepare the dish, the only variation I have noticed is whether white wine or brandy is used when sautéing the calamari. Everyone does agree that the best way to serve this dish is over a bed of piping hot Spanish White Rice (page 179).

SERVES 4

2 pounds whole squid (about 25 to 28)

STUFFING

¼ cup olive oil

1 small onion, finely diced

2 large garlic cloves, finely diced

2 ounces Bayonne ham or prosciutto, finely diced (about ⅓ cup)

½ cup fine dried bread crumbs

1 teaspoon kosher salt

¼ teaspoon freshly ground white pepper

INK SAUCE

⅓ cup olive oil

1 medium onion, finely chopped

6 garlic cloves, crushed and finely diced

⅓ cup brandy

Reserved stuffed squid

1 cup Veal Stock (page 228)

1 cup Basquaise Sauce (page 232)

Reserved squid ink

2 teaspoons kosher salt

¼ teaspoon *piment d'Espelette*

Spanish White Rice (page 179)

To clean the calamari, first cut off the tentacles above the eyes. Chop them finely, and set aside. Remove the round ink sac lodged in the base of the tentacles by pushing it out. Using the tip of a knife, carefully break the ink sacs into a cup and set aside. Pull the entrails free of the body and discard. Remove the bone from the stomach and discard. Rinse the bodies under cold running water to flush them well. Using your fingers, pull off and discard the mottled skin covering the body.

To make the stuffing, warm ¼ cup olive oil in a medium sauté pan over medium-high heat. Add the onion, garlic, and ham and sauté for 2 to 3 minutes. Add the chopped tentacles and cook for 10 minutes, stirring occasionally. Stir in the bread crumbs, salt, and pepper. Set aside to cool for 10 to 15 minutes.

Preheat the oven to 450 degrees F.

Gently stuff the tubes about two-thirds full, taking care not to break them. Fasten the ends shut with toothpicks and set aside.

To make the ink sauce, warm ⅓ cup olive oil in a large *cazuela* or ovenproof casserole. Add the onion and garlic and sauté for 2 to 3 minutes over medium-high heat. Add the stuffed squid

and the brandy. Cook until the liquid reduces by half. Add the veal stock, Basquaise sauce, reserved squid ink, salt, and *piment* and bring to a boil.

Bake in the oven for 1½ hours. Make sure the calamari remain at least three-quarters covered with sauce while cooking. If the liquid evaporates too quickly, keep adding just enough water to cover the calamari.

Separate the calamari from the sauce and set aside. Strain the sauce through a fine-mesh sieve and season with salt and pepper to taste.

Warm the rice just before serving. Spoon a mound of rice in the center of each plate. Lay the stuffed calamari on top, and spoon the sauce over them.

TIP: *You can sometimes buy squid ink in packets at the fish shop if you do not want to save and empty the ink sacs as you clean the squid. Also, be sure not to overstuff the squid or they might break open while cooking.*

FISH CAKE JUAN MARI

If there were a hierarchy of Basque chefs, Juan Mari Arzak of Arzak, just outside San Sebastián, would hold the top rung. And he would be the first to repudiate such a hierarchy, for he is above all a humble man who does what he does because he was born into it and because he loves it. Arzak's grandfather opened what was essentially a roadhouse, and his mother turned it into a popular neighborhood gathering place. Juan Mari has since managed the impossible, earning three Michelin stars and holding on to them longer than any restaurant in Spain, while retaining his local clientele. Solidly planted in what he calls "my sea, my coast, my country," Arzak cooks for "his people," his neighbors and countrymen. Any new dish, no matter how good he and his daughter Elena (also a chef at Arzak) think it may be, must win approval from his people's critical palates before it goes on the menu. Arzak's profound loyalty and passion for his very specific locality translates into an abundant popularity. While I was writing this book, I accompanied Arzak to San Sebastián's La Brecha market. Everyone gave him a bellowing hello, including the policemen, cabdrivers, and each and every vendor in the marketplace. He is extremely well known throughout Spain from his newspaper and magazine articles and television appearances. He gave me this recipe, which is so like the man himself—simple, full of authentic flavor and irresistible charm.

SERVES 6 TO 8

1 pound rock cod fillet, free of bones

Kosher salt

Freshly ground white pepper

2 tablespoons (¼ stick) unsalted butter, melted

2 tablespoons dried bread crumbs

8 large eggs

1 cup Basquaise Sauce (page 232)

1 cup heavy cream

2 teaspoons kosher salt

¼ teaspoon freshly ground white pepper

Sprinkle the fish with salt and pepper.

In a steamer, bring to a simmer a few cups of water, put in the fish, and cook for 6 to 9 minutes, depending on the thickness of the fillet. Using a fork, shred the fish, and remove any remaining visible bones as you work; set aside to cool.

Preheat the oven to 400 degrees F.

Brush the bottom and sides of a 7 × 3½-inch springform mold with the melted butter, then coat the inside of the mold evenly with bread crumbs; set aside.

In a large mixing bowl, whip the eggs to a soft peak. Add the Basquaise sauce, heavy cream, 2 teaspoons salt, and ¼ teaspoon ground pepper. Add the flaked fish, mix the ingredients together well, and pour into the prepared mold.

Place the mold in a roasting pan filled halfway with water and bake in the oven until a knife comes out clean, 1 to 1¼ hours.

Cool slightly before unmolding. Cut into 6 to 8 pieces. May be served warm or cold.

Juan Mari Arzak and Elena Arzak Espina relaxing after service in their century-old Restaurant Arzak in San Sebastián.

WARM CODFISH AND POTATO SALAD

Bakalao Beroa Lursagar Entsaladarekin

This is Basque comfort food. For as long as I can remember, my father made his codfish and potato salad almost every day during Lent. I am convinced my parents loved this salad more than their religion, especially since my father fancied himself an atheist! Cod (the salt cod is desalted before cooking by soaking for approximately 2 days) and potatoes make a wonderfully satisfying combination and a great dish for a summer picnic.

SERVES 4 TO 6

1 ¼ pounds salt cod

12 small Yukon Gold potatoes

4 cups water

1 bouquet garni

1 tablespoon black peppercorns

1 tablespoon freshly squeezed lemon juice

4 tablespoons extra-virgin olive oil

½ teaspoon kosher salt

¼ teaspoon freshly ground white pepper

Pinch of *piment d'Espelette*

1 green Anaheim chile, seeded and finely julienned

1 large shallot, finely sliced

¼ teaspoon crushed coriander seeds

1 tablespoon chopped fresh parsley

3 tablespoons stemmed fresh chervil

Soak the salt cod in cold water to cover for 24 to 48 hours, changing the water 3 to 4 times, to desalt it according to taste.

When cod is ready, place the potatoes in a saucepan, cover with water, and bring to a boil over high heat. Cook until tender, about 20 minutes.

Remove any visible bones from the codfish.

In another large saucepan, bring 4 cups of water to a boil. Add the bouquet garni, peppercorns, and cod and return to a boil. Remove the pan from the heat and set aside for 3 to 4 minutes.

To make the dressing, place the lemon juice, olive oil, salt, pepper, and *piment d'Espelette* in a small bowl and whisk together well; set aside.

As soon as the potatoes are done, cut them into ¼-inch-thick slices, and place them in a large mixing bowl. Add the Anaheim chile, shallot, coriander, and parsley.

Remove the codfish from the cooking water, and discard the water. Break up the codfish, removing any remaining visible bones as you work. Pat it dry and flake it into the mixing bowl. Pour the dressing into the bowl, and gently toss the ingredients until evenly coated. Season with salt and pepper to taste. Garnish with chervil.

HALIBUT CHEEKS WITH GARLIC AND PARSLEY

Halibut Kokotxak Baratxuri-Perresilekin

Fish "cheeks" were popularized by fishermen who, after cleaning the fish, discovered this delicate morsel in the lower jaw of the heads. Boat owners allowed the fishermen to keep the money they could make by selling the fish cheeks on shore. The cheeks constitute a very small part of the fish and are now considered a delicacy—even more so in the Basque country, where *kokotxas* come from the favorite fish, hake. Hake has the advantage of being gelatinous, so the cooking juices naturally thicken and emulsify into a smooth sauce. Halibut is less so, but the results will still be delicious.

SERVES 4 TO 6

2 pounds halibut cheeks, cut in 1-inch cubes

Kosher salt

Freshly ground white pepper

½ cup olive oil

8 garlic cloves, finely sliced

¾ cup Vegetable Stock (page 229) or canned vegetable broth

½ cup chopped fresh parsley

Sprinkle the halibut cheeks with salt and pepper; set aside.

Warm the oil and garlic in an enamel cast-iron pan over medium heat until the garlic turns light brown, about 2 minutes. Transfer the oil and garlic to a bowl; set aside.

Add the halibut cheeks and vegetable stock to the same pan and cook over medium heat until the liquid begins to boil. As soon as it boils, begin swirling the pan in a rapid circular motion with one hand, while slowly adding the reserved oil and garlic with the other hand. Continue swirling the pan to emulsify the ingredients, 1 to 2 minutes. Stir in the parsley and serve immediately.

PEPPERS STUFFED WITH SALT COD

Biperrak Makallaoz Beteta

I have stuffed peppers with crab, goat cheese, and even beans, but the version that is closest to my heart is this one, stuffed with salt cod that has been soaked for about 2 days to remove most of the salt. (You could also substitute fresh cod, if you prefer.)

In any discussion of Basque cuisine, this dish is always mentioned as a signature dish of the region. The best version I have tasted is that of Firmin Arrambide, whose Michelin two-star restaurant, Les Pyrénées, is located in the picturesque town of St.-Jean-Pied-de-Port in Basse Navarre province. There the peppers would be the roasted *piquillo* peppers of Lodosa, which can be found canned in specialty markets in this country.

SERVES 4

1 pound salt cod

¾ cup olive oil

1 large onion, finely diced

4 cloves garlic, minced

1 dried New Mexican chile pepper, seeded and cut into ½-inch pieces

Kosher salt

Freshly ground white pepper

12 roasted *piquillo* peppers (page 19) or 4 roasted red bell peppers, peeled and cored (page 233)

1 cup flour

2 eggs, lightly beaten

2 cups fine dried bread crumbs

1 tablespoon chopped fresh parsley

Soak the salt cod in cold water to cover for 24 to 48 hours, changing the water 3 to 4 times, to desalt according to taste.

Drain and pat the codfish dry. Fillet it into 5 to 6 large pieces and set aside.

Heat ½ cup olive oil in a large sauté pan over medium-high heat. Add the onion, garlic, and chile; sweat until soft and translucent, about 5 minutes. Add the cod fillets, reduce the heat slightly, and cook for 5 minutes, swirling the pan occasionally.

Increase the heat slightly and cook for 5 more minutes, continuing to move the pan in a circular motion every few minutes to emulsify the ingredients. Pour into a colander suspended over a bowl to drain. Reserve the cooking liquid (*jus*) and set aside. Remove and discard the chile pepper. Season with salt and pepper to taste.

Gently smash together the onion and cod, using the back of a large spoon. Remove any remaining bones as you work.

Gently fill the peppers with the cod stuffing until full, taking care not to break the peppers; set aside.

Preheat the oven to 400 degrees F.

Over medium-high heat warm the remaining ¼ cup olive oil in an ovenproof sauté pan.

Dredge the peppers in the flour, dip them into the beaten eggs, then roll them in the bread crumbs. Place the peppers in the sauté pan and brown them on one side for 2 to 3 minutes. Turn them over and put the pan in the oven until the peppers are hot through and golden brown all over, 5 to 7 minutes.

Warm the cod *jus* in a small saucepan over high heat. Add the parsley and swirl the pan until the *jus* boils.

Place a pepper in the center of each plate. Spoon the cod *jus* evenly around the peppers. Garnish with a few turns of the pepper mill.

TIP: *Coating the peppers with bread crumbs is not essential or even traditional. However, I feel it brings an extra dimension to the dish, creating another layer of flavor and texture.*

SALT COD "AL PIL-PIL"

Makallaoa Pil-pilean

This dish is a pillar of Basque cuisine. It is served in just about every home and restaurant, with few variations in the preparation. (Again, the salt cod is presoaked up to 2 days to desalt it.) The name "pil-pil" comes from the sound the bubbling oil makes as the dish cooks in its *cazuela*. In the Basque country there is a saying that salt cod "al pil-pil" is "best when cooked by a man." Supposedly, a man's strength is required for the continuous rotation of the cooking pan necessary to emulsify the sauce. Actually, it takes just a few minutes, but what might be more important is that the skin be left on the cod. The natural gelatin in the skin and the rotating motion of the pan together create this dish.

SERVES 4 TO 6

2 pounds salt cod, skin on
½ cup olive oil
6 garlic cloves, sliced
1 small onion, thinly sliced
½ teaspoon dried chile flakes

Soak the cod in cold water to cover for 24 to 48 hours in the refrigerator, changing the water 3 or 4 times. Drain and pat dry.

Cut the fish into 4 to 6 fillets.

Warm the olive oil, garlic, onion, and chile flakes in a *cazuela* or a large, round shallow casserole over high heat. When the garlic starts to brown, remove it from the pan along with half of the oil; set aside in a small bowl.

Add the cod, skin side up, and simmer over medium heat for 20 minutes, swirling the pan in a rapid regular circular motion every 2 to 3 minutes for 10 to 15 seconds each time to emulsify the ingredients. The sauce should develop into a white, creamy texture. Increase the heat to medium-high and slowly add the reserved garlic oil while simultaneously swirling the pan. Continue the circular motion until the sauce has completely emulsified, about 2 minutes longer.

FRESH CODFISH WITH BASQUAISE SAUCE

Bakalao Euskualdun Saltsarekin

Basques love fresh cod almost as much as salt cod. It is usually treated very simply, not only because of its delicate flavor but because the fish itself can be fragile and difficult to handle. Cod is sometimes steamed and served with lemon or poached and served with a little olive oil drizzled over it. In this recipe, I start the fish off in a hot pan, then add Basquaise sauce, and finish the fillets in the oven. This reduces handling to a minimum and keeps the fish moist as well.

SERVES 4

2 tablespoons olive oil

4 fillets fresh cod
  (about 2 pounds)

Kosher salt

Freshly ground white pepper

1 cup Basquaise Sauce
  (page 232)

2 tablespoons chopped fresh
  parsley

Preheat the oven to 450 degrees F.

Warm the olive oil in a large ovenproof sauté pan over high heat.

Season both sides of the fillets with salt and pepper.

When the oil is hot but not smoking, add the fillets. Sauté on one side until browned, about 5 minutes. Turn the fish over, add the Basquaise sauce, and place directly in the oven until the fillets break under the pressure of your finger, 6 to 8 minutes. Garnish with parsley.

TIP: *If desired, firm the cod before cooking for easier handling. Sprinkle it lightly with salt and let it rest 30 minutes. Then rinse the fish and pat dry with paper towels before cooking.*

HAKE SAN SEBASTIÁN STYLE

Koxkera is the name given to people born in the neighborhood of Calle 31 Augusto (August Thirty-first Street), the oldest street in San Sebastián. It lies in the heart of the *parte vieja* (old quarter) and alone escaped the great fire that destroyed the town in 1813 as the French and Spanish fought for control of the region. *Koxkera* not only evokes the narrow street with its ancient houses and bustling bars, restaurants, and gastronomic societies but also implies continued vitality, endurance, and joy in the face of adversity, as well as an unshakable commitment to Basque traditions. It was the *koxkera* who invented this dish of hake cooked in garlic and parsley. You will find it served in homes and restaurants in San Sebastián and all over the Basque country. Hake is a member of the cod family but smaller and firmer in texture. It is found in both the Atlantic and the Pacific but is probably most prized in the Basque country, where freshness and simplicity of cooking are hallmarks of great hake dishes. Often salt, pepper, and few drops of oil are the only additions to the fish cooked on a hot griddle. If you cannot find hake, look for lingcod or rock cod.

SERVES 4

4 hake steaks, 1 inch thick (about 6 ounces each)

Kosher salt

Freshly ground white pepper

Flour for dredging

¼ cup olive oil

2 teaspoons minced garlic

⅓ cup chopped fresh parsley

¾ cup dry white wine

¾ cup shelled green peas

16 Manila clams

3 hard-boiled eggs, coarsely chopped

12 spears white or green asparagus, cooked and trimmed to 3 inches

2 tablespoons unsalted butter

Season both sides of the fish steaks with salt and pepper. Dredge them in the flour, and set aside.

Warm the olive oil in a large sauté pan or *cazuela* over high heat. Add the steaks, and sauté for 1½ minutes on each side. Remove the fish from the pan, and set aside.

Fish stall at the La Brecha market in San Sebastián.

Add the minced garlic and chopped parsley. Sauté for 1 minute.

Return the fish steaks to the pan and add the white wine, peas, clams, hard-boiled eggs, and asparagus. Bring to a slow boil. Cover and reduce the heat slightly. Cook until the codfish steaks are cooked through and the clams are fully opened, 6 to 8 minutes, discarding any clams that don't open. Transfer the fish to a serving platter or onto individual plates.

Add the butter to the pan and swirl the ingredients in a constant circular motion until the butter has melted and the sauce has bonded slightly. Pour the sauce on top of the fish and serve immediately.

SEA BREAM WITH GARLIC VINAIGRETTE "À LA CONCHA"

This very popular dish from the Spanish Basque coast has been enthusiastically embraced in French Basque country. It is served in many family-style restaurants where grilling is a specialty. In my hometown of Anglet between Bayonne and Biarritz, there is a very popular, large seaside restaurant called La Concha. This dish is its bestseller. Sea bream (daurade) is at its peak in December and January and is commonly part of Basque Christmas celebrations. This simple preparation works well with a wide range of fish and shellfish, such as mussels, sea bass, or halibut.

SERVES 2

2 sea breams (about 1 pound each), cleaned, heads on, or four 5-ounce fillets

Kosher salt

Freshly ground white pepper

5 tablespoons olive oil

4 garlic cloves, finely sliced

1 tablespoon coarsely chopped dried New Mexican chile or ¼ teaspoon dried chile flakes

1½ teaspoons sherry vinegar

Preheat the broiler. Sprinkle the outside of the fish with salt and pepper.

Place the fish under the broiler for 5 minutes. Turn them over and broil for another 5 minutes. Transfer to a serving platter. Run the tip of a knife along the back of the fish to fully open it and remove the central bone. (If you use fillets instead of a whole fish, you should need to broil them only for a total of 5 minutes, skin side up.)

Combine the olive oil and garlic in a small saucepan over medium-high heat just until the garlic turns golden brown, 1 to 2 minutes. Add the chile and the sherry vinegar and swirl the mixture together before pouring it over the fish.

SOLE BRAISED WITH CÈPES AND TXAKOLI

Mihiarraina eta Ondioak Txakolinarekin

This is a variation on a classic French dish and provides a wonderful excuse for showing off one of my favorite white wines, *txakoli*. It is a dry, crisp, slightly pétillant white wine produced in Guetaria, on the coast of Guipúzcoa province. The vineyards grow on steep slopes that fall directly into the sea. On a visit in 1997, Ernesto Chueka, the owner of Txomin Etxaniz Winery, one of the top *txakoli* producers, proudly described how Juan Carlos, king of Spain, wanted to serve Txomin *txakoli* at the wedding of his eldest daughter to a Basque sportsman. But the entire year's production was already sold out! After many telephone calls to understanding restaurants and customers, Chueka gathered enough wine for the occasion. If you cannot find *txakoli* (but I hope you can, as it carries the essence of the Basque coast in its taste), any good-quality fruity white wine will work as well.

SERVES 4

⅓ cup finely chopped shallots

9 tablespoons unsalted butter

1 pound cèpes, stems finely diced and caps sliced into ⅛-inch-thick strips

2 large garlic cloves, minced

Kosher salt

Freshly ground white pepper

8 Dover sole fillets (3 to 4 ounces each) or petrale sole, skin removed

2 cups *txakoli* wine or other fruity white wine

4 tablespoons chopped fresh parsley

1 tablespoon snipped fresh chives

Commemorative bottle of Txomin Etxaniz txakoli served at the wedding of Princess Maria Cristina.

To make the stuffing, sweat the shallots in 2 tablespoons butter in a medium sauté pan over medium heat until translucent, about 3 to 4 minutes. Add the diced mushroom stems and 1 minced garlic clove and cook for 4 to 5 minutes, until the pan is dry. Season with salt and pepper. Spread the stuffing on a sheet pan to cool for 10 minutes.

Preheat the oven to 450 degrees F.

Season the sole with salt and pepper. Spoon 1 to 2 tablespoons of mushroom filling in the center of each fillet, depending on the size of the fish. Roll the fillets around the filling and place them in a *cazuela* or glass baking dish, flap side down.

Scatter any remaining stuffing around the fish. Add the wine and place in the oven until cooked through, about 10 to 12 minutes, depending on the thickness of the sole.

Ernesto Chueka and Gerald Hirigoyen overlooking the txakoli *vineyards in Guetaria.*

Using the same pan the stuffing was prepared in, melt 1 tablespoon butter over high heat. Add the mushroom caps, 1 tablespoon chopped parsley, and the remaining garlic. Sauté until lightly browned, about 4 to 5 minutes. Set aside.

When the fish is done, take the *cazuela* out of the oven and without removing the fish, carefully drain the juices into a small saucepan. Add the remaining 3 tablespoons parsley, chives, and salt and pepper to taste, and bring to a boil. Swirl in the remaining 6 tablespoons butter and whisk vigorously. Spread the mushroom caps over the sole, and pour the sauce on top.

POACHED TROUT WITH TOMATO VINAIGRETTE

Amuarraina Geldiro Egosia Tomaterekin

The century-old hotel-restaurant Arcé perches on the banks of the trout-filled Nive River in the green valley of St.-Etienne-de-Baïgorry near the Spanish border in the Basse Navarre. When a guest orders trout, a *sous-chef*, net in hand, sprints across the patio and disappears underneath. A moment later he emerges with a live trout plucked from the inn's holding tanks in the river. My wife is always so amused by the spectacle that she orders trout each time we go. This dish may be served hot or cold, depending on the weather and your mood.

In a blender or food processor, combine the tomatoes, sherry vinegar, olive oil, pastis, salt, pepper, sugar, and *piment d'Espelette*. Blend just until pureed, about 1 minute; set aside.

In a large casserole, combine the vegetable stock and red wine vinegar and bring to a boil. Sprinkle salt and pepper inside the trout. Once the liquid boils, add the fillets. Return to a boil and cook for 1 minute longer, just enough to poach the fish.

Using a large slotted spoon, remove the trout and set them on a serving platter. Serve with the tomato vinaigrette on the side or spooned across the middle of the fish.

SERVES 4

1 pint cherry tomatoes (such as Sweet 100s) or 2 medium vine-ripened tomatoes

1 tablespoon sherry vinegar

3 tablespoons extra-virgin olive oil

1 tablespoon pastis, such as Ricard or Pernod

1 teaspoon kosher salt

¼ teaspoon freshly ground white pepper

1 teaspoon sugar

Pinch of *piment d'Espelette*

2 quarts Vegetable Stock (page 229) or canned vegetable broth

½ cup red wine vinegar

4 freshwater trout, cleaned, boned, and heads removed (about ½ pound each after cleaning)

Chef Pascal Arcé nabbing a trout from the Nive River.

HALIBUT BRAISED WITH CLAMS IN GREEN PEA SALSA

Halibut Txirlekin Saltsa Leka Berdetan

SERVES 4

30 Manila clams

4 halibut fillets (about ¼ pound each)

Kosher salt

Freshly ground white pepper

1 tablespoon olive oil

2 cups shelled green peas

1 cup Vegetable Stock (page 229) or canned vegetable broth

2 garlic cloves, peeled

⅓ cup dry white wine

1 tablespoon unsalted butter

The four basic sauces of Basque cuisine are known by their colors: white, red, green, and black. Three of the sauce colors are also those of the national flag. This is not surprising in a country that manages to work its flag's colors and design into everything from the paint on the fishing fleets to the careful arrangement of vegetables in a market stall. The white sauce is made of garlic and oil, the black is squid ink, the red includes tomatoes and peppers, and the green (called *salsa verde*) is parsley and garlic. I have never felt that the *salsa verde* looked as green as its name implies, so I created this tasty, very green sauce to accent the dish.

Preheat the oven to 475 degrees F.

Rinse the clams thoroughly under running water. Scatter them in a large, shallow glass baking dish; set aside.

To cook the fillets, sprinkle them on both sides with salt and pepper. In a large nonstick sauté pan over high heat, warm 1 tablespoon olive oil. Place the fillets in the hot pan, and cook just until golden brown on both sides, about 1 minute each side. Transfer the fillets to the dish with the clams.

Puree 1 cup peas, the vegetable stock, the garlic cloves, and the white wine in a blender on high speed. Pour the puree over the fish fillets and place in the oven to bake until the fish is cooked through and the clams have opened fully, 10 to 12 minutes. Discard any clams that don't open.

Transfer fillets to a large serving platter. Remove the clams and set them aside. Strain the sauce into a large shallow sauté pan and place over high heat. Swirl in butter and add the remaining cup of peas. Season with salt and pepper to taste and bring to a boil. Cook until peas are just tender, about 3 minutes.

To serve, arrange the clams all around the fish fillets. Pour the pea sauce over the fish.

MONKFISH IN RED WINE WITH LEEKS AND PANCETTA

Monkfish, known as the "toad of the sea" because it is so unattractive, used to be tossed back into the ocean. Now it is prized for its firm, almost meaty texture. One of the classic preparations for monkfish is "à la Bordelaise," meaning that it is cooked in the red wine of Bordeaux. This is a Basque version of that dish using Irouleguy, the rich red wine of Basse Navarre. You could also use a great Rioja. The Rioja is probably the best known wine region of Spain. What is less well known is that it stretches across both the Alava and the Navarra provinces of Basque country.

SERVES 4

1 tablespoon olive oil

6 ounces pancetta, cut in ¼-inch-thick strips (about 1 cup)

1 medium leek, trimmed and julienned

1 bouquet garni

2 cups dry red wine

2 pounds monkfish or salmon fillets

Kosher salt

Freshly ground white pepper

3 tablespoons unsalted butter

2 tablespoons chopped fresh parsley

Preheat the oven to 450 degrees F.

Warm the olive oil in a large sauté pan over high heat.

Add the pancetta, and sauté until golden brown and crispy, 2 to 3 minutes. Add leek and bouquet garni; sauté for 1 to 2 minutes. Add the red wine and bring to a boil. Cook until the liquid reduces by half.

Slice the monkfish into ¾-inch-thick medallions. Season the fish with salt and pepper.

Add the monkfish to the pan and place in the oven to bake for 3 to 4 minutes. Turn the medallions over, and bake until the fish is cooked through and firm to the touch, about 4 to 5 minutes longer.

Transfer the fish to a platter. Discard the bouquet garni.

Return the pan to high heat, and bring the liquid to a boil. Swirl in 3 tablespoons butter. Add parsley and season with salt and pepper to taste. Pour the sauce over the monkfish and serve immediately.

BAKED SALMON FILLET WITH RED PEPPER SABAYON

Izokina Erreta Biperrekin

SERVES 4

Kosher salt

Freshly ground white pepper

1¼ pounds salmon fillet

2 tablespoons olive oil

2 small red bell peppers, roasted, peeled, and cored, or 4 roasted *piquillo* peppers (page 233)

⅓ cup Vegetable Stock (page 229) or canned vegetable broth

¼ teaspoon *piment d'Espelette*

5 egg yolks

1 tablespoon water

1 tablespoon roasted, seeded, and diced red bell pepper or roasted, diced *piquillo* pepper (page 233)

1 tablespoon chopped fresh parsley

When I was about nine years old, my father decided to take up fishing. Off we went salmon fishing in the Adour River, which flows east of Bayonne. Now my father was a great man, and an even greater cook, but truth be told, he was not a fisherman. I think he spent more time with his lines out of the water than in, and I don't recall that he ever caught a fish. On our way home, we would stop at a riverside restaurant, where we invariably ordered salmon. It wasn't long before my father threw away his fishing pole, but we continued to drive out to the river for years just to dine on freshly caught salmon. If I were to make that drive today, my first stop would be the Michelin two-star Auberge de la Galupe in the small town of Urt. The restaurant occupies an old countryside manor on the banks of the Adour where Christian Parra, a passionate adherent of local products, presides over the stove.

Preheat the oven to 450 degrees F.

Sprinkle salt and pepper on both sides of the fillets.

In a rectangular baking dish, combine the olive oil and salmon, and bake until the salmon is firm to the touch and pink inside, 15 to 18 minutes. It should not be cooked through. Remove the salmon from the oven and drain and discard the excess liquid from the pan. Increase the oven temperature to broil.

To make the sabayon, combine the whole roasted peppers, vegetable stock, *piment d'Espelette*, and salt and pepper to taste in a blender on high speed until smooth and frothy, about 30 seconds. Pour this coulis into a small saucepan and place it over medium heat.

In the top of a double boiler, over simmering water, vigorously whisk together the egg yolks and 1 tablespoon water until frothy and slightly stiff, 3 to 4 minutes.

Immediately whisk one-third of the warm coulis into the egg mixture. Add the remaining coulis and whisk constantly until the ingredients are smooth and evenly combined, 2 to 3 minutes. You should have about 1 cup of sabayon.

Stir the diced pepper and parsley into the sabayon and coat the top of the salmon with it. Return the salmon to the uppermost rack in the oven to broil until the sabayon is slightly browned on top, 2 to 3 minutes.

Bayonne.

SEARED AHI TUNA STEAKS WITH ONION MARMALADE

This dish was inspired by my uncle's tuna and onion casserole. He would put a big tuna steak in a casserole and cover it with onions and a little oil. Then he cooked it on top of the stove for a long, long time. When I came to California and tasted ahi tuna cooked rare like a steak, I was hooked. So I adapted my uncle's combination of ingredients to the West Coast cooking style. This same preparation, served on a steaming bed of green lentils, was the most popular dish on the opening menu at Fringale in 1991. Every time I tried to retire it, the customers would stage an uproar.

SERVES 4

ONION MARMALADE

¼ cup olive oil

2 large onions, finely sliced

¼ cup sherry vinegar

½ cup balsamic vinegar

½ cup water

1 teaspoon kosher salt

¼ teaspoon freshly ground white pepper

1 teaspoon sugar

¼ teaspoon *piment d'Espelette*

1 tablespoon olive oil

4 tuna steaks (about 6 ounces each and 1½ inches thick)

Kosher salt

Freshly ground white pepper

2 cups warm Green Lentils with Bacon (page 176)

To make the onion marmalade, warm ¼ cup olive oil in a medium sauté pan over medium-high heat. Add the onions and sauté until they turn golden brown, about 10 minutes. Stir in the vinegars, water, 1 teaspoon salt, ¼ teaspoon pepper, sugar, and *piment d'Espelette*. Bring to a slow boil and cook until the liquid is completely evaporated, about 15 minutes. Remove from the heat and set aside.

In a separate medium-large sauté pan, warm 1 tablespoon olive oil over medium-high heat. Sprinkle both sides of the tuna steaks with salt and pepper. Sear them until medium rare, about 2 minutes on each side, depending on the thickness of the tuna.

For each serving, spoon the lentils onto the center of a plate. Place a tuna steak on top and cover with onion marmalade.

CRAB AND POTATO GRATIN

Piled high in its own cleaned shells, *txangurro* (stuffed spider crab) makes one of the most evocative dishes of the Basque coastal region. The spider crab has very long legs but no claws, and is found all along the coast. This recipe challenges tradition by the addition of potatoes, but I like the way they offset the richness of the crab. As a result, I've dubbed this dish my "Shepherd's Pie of the Sea." If you are cooking and cleaning your own crab to make this dish, reserve the shells to use for presentation. Otherwise, I like to use a *cazuela,* or earthenware serving dish.

SERVES 4 TO 6

1 ½ pounds russet potatoes, peeled and coarsely chopped

6 garlic cloves

½ cup warm milk

8 tablespoons (1 stick) unsalted butter

2 tablespoons olive oil

⅓ cup finely diced onion

⅓ cup diced roasted red bell peppers (page 233)

1 pound fresh crabmeat

½ cup dry white wine

3 tablespoons snipped fresh chives

3 tablespoons chopped fresh basil

Kosher salt

Freshly ground white pepper

¼ teaspoon *piment d'Espelette*

3 tablespoons fine dried bread crumbs

Preheat the broiler.

Place the potatoes and garlic cloves in a large saucepan. Cover with water, and bring to a boil. Cook until soft throughout, 15 to 20 minutes. Drain, spread them on a sheet pan, and place under the broiler to "dry out" for 2 to 3 minutes.

Scoop potatoes and garlic into a food mill and grind over a large bowl (or mash the potatoes and garlic together, using a large fork). Stir in the milk and 6 tablespoons butter; set aside.

Warm the olive oil in a large sauté pan. Add the onion and pepper and sauté until translucent, 4 to 5 minutes.

Add the crab and white wine, and bring to a boil. Cook until the wine has evaporated completely. Remove from the heat, add the chives and basil, and season with salt and pepper to taste. Add the *piment d'Espelette* and mix the ingredients together well.

Place the mixture in an ovenproof *cazuela,* or in four individual crab shells.

Sprinkle the bread crumbs evenly over the top of the crab and potato mixture and dot with the remaining 2 tablespoons butter on top. Place under the broiler until the surface is lightly browned, 6 to 8 minutes.

SAUTÉED PRAWNS IN PASTIS WITH LEMON AND CHERRY TOMATOES

The Basque region commands the passes through the Pyrenees on the Atlantic side of the peninsula, and the Basques know their mountains intimately. Ever since there were borders in those mountains, Basques have made smuggling an honorable profession, never committing contracts to writing, and always achieving their goal. My family and neighbors participated in this age-old occupation in a small way by smuggling bottles of pastis across the border from Spain, where it was far less expensive. People on the French side of the border would brag about how many contraband bottles they had stockpiled. My parents used to hide the pastis under my sister and me, or in a hidden spot in the trunk of the car, or transfer the pastis to wine bottles. We held our breath as we passed through the border, petrified by the guards with their shiny black hats and long rifles. It wasn't until the checkpoint was a tiny speck in the rearview mirror that we would finally exhale. Still, I am captivated by pastis, to the extent that my partner and I named our second San Francisco restaurant after it!

SERVES 4

2 tablespoons olive oil

1¼ pounds shrimp (about 25; 16-20s means 16 to 20 shrimp per pound), shelled and deveined

10 ounces cherry tomatoes, cut in half

3 tablespoons pastis, such as Ricard or Pernod

3 tablespoons freshly squeezed lemon juice

8 tablespoons (1 stick) unsalted butter, cut into small pieces

2 tablespoons julienned fresh basil

1 tablespoon chopped fresh parsley

1 tablespoon snipped fresh chives

Kosher salt

Freshly ground white pepper

Warm the olive oil in a large sauté pan over high heat.

Add the shrimp and sauté for about 2 minutes, stirring frequently.

Add the tomatoes and the pastis, then flambé until the flame dies out.

Add the lemon juice, butter, basil, parsley, and chives and season with salt and pepper to taste. Swirl the pan over the heat just until the butter is completely melted into the sauce. Take care not to boil, or the sauce may separate.

SEAFOOD AND SHELLFISH STEW

Ttoro

In the old days, people made a "fish" soup by adding a few vegetables to the cooking liquid left after poaching salt cod. From that humble beginning blossomed St.-Jean-de-Luz's sumptuous seafood soup brimming with rockfish, langoustine, mussels, and sometimes monkfish. It occupies the same place in Basque cuisine as bouillabaisse does in Provence. If you are ever in the vicinity of Socoa, just across from St.-Jean-de-Luz in Labourd, be sure to stop in at Pantxua. It is one of the best fish restaurants along the coast. The stove is "manned" by Madame Hou, who in my opinion makes one of the best *ttoros* on earth.

SERVES 4 TO 6

FISH BROTH

1 onion, coarsely chopped

1 carrot, coarsely chopped

2 medium celery stalks, coarsely chopped

1 small leek, trimmed and coarsely chopped

12 garlic cloves, crushed

⅓ cup olive oil

3 pounds fish heads and trimmings

2 cups dry white wine

8 cups water

3 tomatoes, cored and quartered

1 bouquet garni

1 dried chile pepper, seeded and halved

1 tablespoon black peppercorns

CROUTONS

½ day-old baguette

1 garlic clove

4 ounces dried sheep's milk cheese or Swiss cheese, grated

TO MAKE THE BROTH

In a stockpot or casserole, combine the onion, carrot, celery, leek, garlic, and olive oil over medium heat. Sauté until the vegetables begin to brown, about 5 minutes.

Add the fish heads and trimmings. Cover, and cook for 10 minutes, skimming the top occasionally.

Add the wine. Cook until it reduces by half, about 8 minutes.

Add the water, tomatoes, bouquet garni, chile pepper, and peppercorns. Bring to a boil. Reduce heat, and let simmer for 45 minutes to 1 hour. Strain, and set aside.

TO MAKE THE CROUTONS

Preheat the oven to 450 degrees F.

Cut the baguette into 24 slices, about ⅓ inch thick. Rub both sides of each piece of bread with the garlic clove. Sprinkle the cheese evenly over the top of the bread slices.

Place in the oven until the surface is golden brown, 5 to 6 minutes.

SOUP

⅓ cup olive oil

1 pound fresh hake fillet, cut in thick medallions

1 pound boneless monkfish fillet, cut in thick medallions

Kosher salt

Freshly ground white pepper

1 cup flour

8 cups fish broth (see above) or clam juice

1 pound mussels, washed and bearded

1 pound Manila clams, well scrubbed

4 to 6 langoustines (preferably with heads attached)

TO MAKE THE SOUP

Preheat oven to 500 degrees F.

Warm the olive oil to sizzling in a large sauté pan. Sprinkle the hake and monkfish medallions with salt and pepper, and dredge in the flour. First add the monkfish to the sauté pan. Brown on each side for 1 to 2 minutes. Remove and drain on paper towels. Repeat with the hake.

Bring the fish broth to a boil. Add the monkfish, hake, mussels, clams, and langoustines to the broth. Cover, and put in the oven to cook for 5 to 7 minutes. Season with salt and pepper to taste and serve in large soup bowls, garnished with several croutons.

Ttoro *served at Restaurant Pantxua.*

POULTRY AND GAME

BREAST OF TURKEY STUFFED WITH CHESTNUTS AND CHANTERELLES

Roast turkey for holiday meals is more than an American phenomenon. As I was growing up, my mother served turkey and chestnuts for our Christmas dinner. Many variations of the dish exist, but this recipe is one of the most traditional. For my first Thanksgiving in the United States, friends elected me to cook. They didn't pay much attention until they noticed the lack of mashed potatoes and cranberry sauce. Only after they tasted the wonderful chestnut stuffing, sautéed turkey liver, and fresh vegetables did their brows unfurrow. Stuffing the breast is a terrific preparation for turkey because it produces beautiful slices, keeps the meat moist, and makes the best sandwiches. And feel free to add cranberry sauce to your menu if you like.

SERVES 8

One 6-pound boneless whole turkey breast

1½ cups heavy cream

Kosher salt

Freshly ground white pepper

2 egg whites

½ cup plus 1 tablespoon olive oil

½ pound chanterelles

½ pound Roasted Chestnuts, halved (page 236)

¼ cup shelled pistachio nuts

2 tablespoons chopped fresh parsley

2 large carrots, coarsely chopped

2 medium onions, coarsely chopped

2 medium celery stalks, coarsely chopped

2 cups dry white wine

2 cups water

String

Preheat the oven to 375 degrees F.

Lay the meat skin side down and trim off the 2 large fillets attached to each side of the breast. Cut the fillets into small cubes and set aside.

Trim a few layers of meat off the edge of each breast and use them to fill in the cavity between the double breasts in order to create a somewhat flat surface.

In a food processor fitted with a metal blade, combine the cubed turkey fillets and the heavy cream. Pulse a few times to break down the meat, then begin mixing on low speed. Add about 1 teaspoon salt, ¼ teaspoon pepper, and the egg whites and blend just until the forcemeat is smooth; set aside in the refrigerator.

Overlooking Guetaria.

Warm 1 tablespoon olive oil in a large sauté pan over medium-high heat. Add the chanterelles and a pinch of salt and pepper. Sauté until the mushrooms are just wilted, 2 to 3 minutes. Remove from the heat and let cool for 10 minutes.

In a large mixing bowl, combine the forcemeat, chestnuts, pistachios, parsley, and mushrooms. Mix well. Season the turkey with salt and pepper, then spread the stuffing in an even layer on top of the meat. Roll the turkey up as tightly as possible. If there is extra skin on the ends, try to pull the flaps around the meat. Tie up the roast in several places with kitchen string.

Place in a roasting pan, seam side facing down, and sprinkle with salt and pepper. Pour remaining ½ cup olive oil on top of the meat and scatter the carrots, onions, and celery around the pan. Roast in the oven for 15 minutes, then add the white wine to the pan. Return to the oven to cook for 30 minutes, then add 2 cups of water to the pan. Continue to cook until the turkey is done, about 45 minutes longer, basting the bird every 10 to 15 minutes. (It should have an internal temperature of at least 185 degrees on an instant-reading thermometer.)

Transfer the roast to a cutting board. Strain the pan juices into a small saucepan and discard the vegetables. Place the juices over medium-high heat, and skim off any visible fat. Season with salt and pepper to taste. Slice the turkey into ½-inch-thick slices, and serve with the warmed pan juices on the side.

ROASTED CHICKEN "IROULEGUY"

Oilasko Errekia Irulegiko

My family often ate chicken for our midday meal. When my father roasted a bird, he deglazed the pan with red wine to make a sauce. I've taken his idea a little further by creating a compound butter with the Basque Irouleguy wine. It gives the chicken great flavor and color. The butter also flavors the stuffing, which tastes so incredibly delicious and is so easy to make that you may adopt the method for all your stuffings! The butter is also good on top of a juicy steak, too. Serve the chicken with Fried Garlic Potatoes (page 168).

SERVES 4 TO 6

- 2 cups Irouleguy or other dry red wine
- 2/3 cup finely diced shallots
- 12 tablespoons (1½ sticks) unsalted butter, at room temperature
- 1 teaspoon kosher salt
- Pinch of freshly ground white pepper
- 1 roasting chicken (about 5 pounds)
- ½ loaf day-old crusty bread, cut into 1-inch cubes
- 1 cup water
- Kitchen string

Simmer the wine and shallots in a small saucepan over medium heat until the liquid evaporates completely, 35 to 40 minutes.

Place the butter in a medium-size mixing bowl. Add the red wine–shallot mixture, salt, and pepper. Using a wire whisk or wooden spoon, combine the ingredients. Place in the refrigerator to harden for at least 1 hour.

Preheat the oven to 450 degrees F.

Rinse the chicken with water and pat it dry with paper towels. Rub it inside and out with salt and pepper to taste. Without tearing or puncturing the skin, slip your fingers between the skin and the flesh to detach (but not remove) the skin from the body of the chicken. Rub half of the red wine–shallot butter all over the chicken underneath the skin.

Coat the croutons with half the remaining butter and stuff them inside the chicken cavity. Tie the chicken legs together and then tie the legs and wings tightly to the body.

Place the chicken in a roasting pan and smear the remaining butter mixture all over the top.

Roast the chicken for 20 minutes. Add 1 cup of water to the pan. Continue to roast, basting occasionally, until the juices run clear when the thigh is pierced with a knife, about 40 minutes longer. (The internal temperature should be at least 185 degrees on an instant-reading thermometer.)

Transfer the chicken from the roasting pan to a cutting board.

Snip the trussing strings and discard them. Remove the bread from the cavity and arrange it around the edge of a serving platter or in a separate bowl. Carve the chicken, and place it in the center of the platter, spooning gravy on and around the chicken. Serve immediately.

TIP: *While it's important to let red meat rest before carving, I like to carve chicken as soon as it comes from the oven. The skin is still crisp, and if you wait, you risk losing that crispness. Crispy skin is possibly my favorite part of the chicken.*

POULET BASQUAISE

Oilasko Eskualdun

This dish exemplifies the simplicity of Basque cuisine. It coaxes the most flavor possible out of very few ingredients, creating a dish that is more than the sum of its parts. It is a dish we had often as I grew up, and it is one that we make frequently as a staff meal in my restaurants. It has a wonderful, satisfying, savory character that makes anyone who eats it feel well cared for.

SERVES 4

One 5-pound chicken

Flour for dredging

½ cup olive oil

4½ ounces thickly sliced pancetta, coarsely chopped (about ¾ cup)

1 medium onion, thinly sliced

3 large red bell peppers, peeled, cored, and thinly sliced

10 garlic cloves, crushed

6 medium tomatoes (about 2 pounds), cored and coarsely chopped

1 bouquet garni

1 tablespoon kosher salt

¼ teaspoon freshly ground white pepper

¼ teaspoon *piment d'Espelette*

Cut the chicken into quarters: each breast half should be in three parts (the breast in 2 pieces and part of the breast still attached to the wings), and the drumsticks separated from the thighs. Discard the carcass or store it in the freezer for making chicken stock at a later time. Dredge the chicken pieces in flour and set aside.

Warm ¼ cup olive oil in an 8-quart saucepan over medium-high heat.

Working in two batches, sauté the chicken and the pancetta together just long enough to brown the poultry on both sides, about 5 minutes for each batch. Remove the ingredients from the pan and set aside. Discard any remaining fat from the pan. Add the remaining ¼ cup olive oil to the same pan over medium-high heat. Add the onion, peppers, and garlic; sauté for 5 minutes. Add the chicken and pancetta, tomatoes, bouquet garni, salt, pepper, and *piment d'Espelette.* Cover and reduce the heat to medium. Cook until the chicken is cooked through, about 15 to 20 minutes. Remove the breasts and set aside. Finish cooking the remaining ingredients until the thighs are done, about 20 minutes longer. Return the breasts to the pan until warmed through, about 3 to 4 minutes. Remove and discard bouquet garni.

ROASTED DUCK WITH DRIED CHERRIES AND PINE NUTS

Ahate Erreta Gerezieta Pinahaziekin

When we were young, my friends and I used to play in the forest of Anglet, my hometown, and pick nuts from the pinecones we found there. Pine nuts have been one of my favorite nuts ever since, and I use them every chance I get. They are wonderful with meat, in salads, on pasta, or even just to toast and snack on. Choose a young, tender duckling for this recipe. A Peking or Long Island duck would be suitable, not a Moulard or Muscovy. I usually remove the skin before serving, but that is not essential. During cherry season, use the fresh fruit.

SERVES 2 OR 3

1 duckling (about 3 pounds), with neck if available

Kosher salt

Freshly ground white pepper

String

1 tablespoon olive oil

½ cup dry white wine

¼ cup dried cherries (or ½ cup fresh cherries, pitted)

Zest of ½ orange

1 cup Veal Stock (page 228)

¼ cup toasted pine nuts

2 tablespoons (¼ stick) unsalted butter

Preheat the oven to 450 degrees F.

Sprinkle the duck inside and out with salt and pepper, and truss it with kitchen string.

Warm the olive oil in a large ovenproof casserole over high heat. Add the duck (and neck) and sear until browned all over, about 8 minutes.

Place in the oven to roast for 1 hour.

Transfer the duck to a cutting board.

Pour off any fat from the casserole. Deglaze the pan over high heat with the white wine by stirring and scraping the bottom and sides of the pan to loosen any browned bits. Add the dried (or fresh) cherries and orange zest and cook until the wine reduces by half.

Add the stock and bring to a boil. Add the pine nuts and swirl in the butter until evenly incorporated. Season with salt and pepper to taste. Cut the duck into serving pieces. Remove and discard the skin. Return the meat to the sauce just long enough to warm through.

MAGRET OF DUCK SALAD WITH APPLE AND POMEGRANATE

Ahate Ugatza Sagar eta Mingranarekin

The cooking of the French Basque provinces is influenced not only by Spain but also by Gascony, the nearest neighbor to the north. Magret is the breast of a Muscovy or Moulard duck, the large ducks used for foie gras, a specialty of Gascony. The breast is best cooked as you would a steak, then very thinly sliced. The pomegranate seeds add color and their bright, sweet-tart taste makes a tantalizing contrast with the rich taste of the duck. Serve the salad as an elegant lunch, a light supper, or a first course for a dinner party.

SERVES 4 AS A LUNCH OR LIGHT SUPPER DISH; 4 TO 5 AS A FIRST COURSE

- 1 Muscovy duck breast (about 1 pound)
- Kosher salt
- Freshly ground white pepper
- ¼ cup balsamic vinegar
- ½ cup pomegranate juice
- ⅓ cup Veal Stock (page 228)
- 2 tablespoons (¼ stick) unsalted butter
- 1 medium-size tart green apple, peeled, cored, and julienned
- 4 cups loosely packed frisée lettuce
- ¼ cup toasted pine nuts
- 2 tablespoons snipped fresh chives
- 2 tablespoons extra-virgin olive oil
- ¼ cup pomegranate seeds

Preheat the oven to 400 degrees F.

Remove the excess fat around the edges of the duck breast, and incise the remaining skin diagonally and horizontally every inch. Season the breast with salt and pepper, and place it, skin side down, in a medium-large ovenproof sauté pan.

Cook over high heat until the skin begins to brown, 2 to 3 minutes, then place in the oven to cook for another 10 minutes. Turn the breast over, and continue to cook until firm to the touch, about 5 minutes longer for medium rare. Remove the duck and set aside.

Discard the fat from the pan, and deglaze the pan with the balsamic vinegar. Cook until the vinegar is reduced by half. Add the pomegranate juice, reduce it by half, then add the veal stock, and again reduce the liquid by half. Bring to a boil, and continue to cook until the liquid again reduces by half. Season with salt and pepper to taste.

Swirl in the butter. When evenly incorporated, remove from the heat and set aside.

Combine the apple, frisée, pine nuts, chives, and olive oil in a mixing bowl and toss together well. Sprinkle with salt and pepper.

Distribute the salad among four plates, and top with pomegranate seeds.

Slice the duck breast diagonally into ¼-inch-thick slices and arrange, tepee style, on top of each salad. Drizzle the pomegranate reduction around the edge of each plate.

DUCK LEG CONFIT

Confit originally referred to the process of cooking and preserving pork or duck in its own fat. Now we use the term more loosely to refer to anything cooked slowly in a large amount of oil or fat. This simple but time-consuming process of preserving meat is particular to the southwest of France and extends into the French Basque provinces. The best parts of the duck for confit are the legs and wings; the breast tends to dry out. Use Muscovy or Moulard ducks (the legs are marinated overnight with garlic, peppercorns, and herbs), and serve the confit with a generous pile of Fried Garlic Potatoes (page 168) or Green Lentils with Bacon (page 176).

SERVES 4

4 whole duck legs (about ¾ pound each)

1 tablespoon kosher salt

Freshly ground white pepper

12 garlic cloves, crushed

1 tablespoon black peppercorns

4 sprigs fresh thyme, coarsely chopped

2 bay leaves

Rendered Duck Fat (page 231), about 6 cups (3 pounds)

Season the duck with salt and pepper and place it in a shallow container. Scatter the garlic, peppercorns, thyme, and bay leaves on top of the legs. Cover with plastic wrap and refrigerate overnight. Remove from the refrigerator and set aside until the meat reaches room temperature, then pat the meat dry.

Melt the rendered duck fat in a large enameled cast-iron pot over medium heat. When it begins to boil, add the duck, garlic, peppercorns, thyme, and bay leaves. Bring to a boil, reduce the heat to a slow simmer, and cook, uncovered, until the meat is easily pierced with a fork and the juices run clear, about 2¼ to 2½ hours.

Transfer the meat to a deep earthenware bowl or terrine. Strain the fat over the bowl to cover the meat completely. Let cool until the fat hardens. Make sure that the duck pieces are totally sealed in the fat so that no air can reach them. Cover and refrigerate for at least 24 hours or up to 3 weeks.

Preheat the oven to 450 degrees F.

Remove the duck legs from the fat, making sure to wipe away as much excess fat as possible. Place the meat, skin side down, in a roasting pan in the oven until the skin is crispy and the meat is heated through, about 15 minutes. Reserve the fat for general cooking purposes or reuse for additional confit.

Basque flag (L'ikuriña).

CARAMELIZED QUAIL

Pospolin Karamelatua

I remember when, in the late fall, a ragout of small migrating birds was a great treat and delicacy. The birds are hunted without guns. Instead, nets are spread on the ground and the hunters wait for a flock to settle in the field. Then the net is sprung like a trap around the birds. The closest bird commercially available to those migrating birds is the quail. Isabelle Alexandre, our chef at Pastis, has a particular talent with quail, and this is her recipe. Quail are typically served with white beans (page 178) in the Basque country. You can also serve the quail with Green Lentils with Bacon (page 176) or Corn Risotto (page 53).

SERVES 4

4 tablespoons olive oil

3 sprigs chopped fresh thyme

2 teaspoons black peppercorns

2 garlic cloves, finely sliced

4 boneless or partially boned quail (4 to 5 ounces each)

2 teaspoons sugar

1 small shallot, finely diced

⅔ cup dry red wine

½ cup Veal Stock (page 228)

Kosher salt

Freshly ground white pepper

2 tablespoons (¼ stick) unsalted butter

Combine 2 tablespoons olive oil, thyme, black peppercorns, and garlic in a shallow container. Add the quail, coating it thoroughly with the marinade, cover, and set aside in a refrigerator for 2 to 3 hours.

Remove the quail from the refrigerator a half hour before cooking. Sprinkle the skin side of the birds evenly with the sugar.

Warm the remaining 2 tablespoons olive oil in a large sauté pan over medium-high heat. Add the quail, skin side down, and lay a heavy lid or brick wrapped in aluminum foil on top to gently flatten the quail. Cook until caramelized, 3 to 4 minutes. Turn the quail over, and sauté until cooked through, about 2 minutes longer.

Transfer the quail to a warmed platter. Quickly discard the fat from the pan and deglaze the pan with the shallot and red wine by stirring and scraping all over the sides and bottom to loosen the browned bits. Bring to a boil and reduce the wine by half. Add the veal stock, return to a boil, and season with salt and pepper to taste. Swirl in the butter until evenly incorporated. Pour over the quail.

Kosher salt

Freshly ground white
pepper

2 tablespoons chopped fresh
parsley

Discard the fat, and return the pan to high heat. Add the boar and bacon, sprinkle the meat with flour, and sauté for 2 to 3 minutes. Again, transfer the meat to a colander.

Still using the same sauté pan, over high heat, add the remaining 1 tablespoon olive oil and the reserved marinade vegetables. Sauté until they begin to brown, 2 to 3 minutes. Return the meats to the pan and add the reserved red wine marinade. Bring to a boil, add the veal stock, and return to a boil. Reduce the heat to medium and simmer, slowly, uncovered, until the meat is tender throughout, about 2 hours.

Drain the meat and vegetables through a sieve, capturing the sauce in a medium sauté pan, and placing it over medium-high heat.

Separate the meat from the vegetables. Discard the vegetables, the bouquet garni, and the cheesecloth bouquet.

Add the chocolate to the sauce, stir until melted, then swirl the butter into the sauce until it is completely melted. Season with salt and pepper to taste.

Arrange the meat in the center of a platter or on individual plates and spoon the sauce over the meat. Garnish with chopped parsley and serve immediately.

FILLET OF VENISON WITH QUINCE

Hunting has always been popular in the mountainous Basque country to protect animals and crops as well as to provide food and sport. Venison and wild boar were once plentiful enough to be considered local foods and still are widely available.

There is even a venison chorizo. In this savory winter stew the meat is marinated for 24 hours with wine, vegetables, herbs, and seasonings—the basis of its deeply flavored black pepper sauce. The quince puree adds an unexpected flavor and lightness to the dish.

SERVES 4 TO 6

1½ pounds venison fillet, trimmed

2 cups dry red wine

1 medium carrot, coarsely chopped

½ medium celery stalk, coarsely chopped

1 small white onion, coarsely chopped

¼ pound quince, unpeeled, cored, and coarsely chopped

1 tablespoon juniper berries

2 tablespoons black peppercorns

1 bouquet garni

3 garlic cloves, crushed

4 tablespoons olive oil

Kosher salt

Freshly ground white pepper

2 tablespoons brandy

1 teaspoon sherry vinegar

¼ cup Veal Stock (page 228)

2 tablespoons (¼ stick) unsalted butter

1 cup Quince Puree (page 237)

To make the marinade, put the venison in a narrow container. Pour the red wine over the meat, making sure to cover it completely. Add the carrot, celery, onion, quince, juniper berries, 1 tablespoon peppercorns, bouquet garni, crushed garlic, and 1 tablespoon olive oil. Cover with plastic wrap and refrigerate for 24 hours.

Preheat the oven to 475 degrees F.

Separate the venison and bouquet garni from the marinade and set aside. Strain the marinade into a large saucepan and set aside the vegetables. Bring the marinade to a boil with the bouquet garni.

In a sauté pan, warm 1 tablespoon olive oil over high heat. Add the vegetables from the marinade and sauté until they start to brown, 3 to 4 minutes. Pour the boiling marinade into the pan with the vegetables and reduce the heat to medium. Cook until the marinade reduces by half. Strain the reduction, reserve the liquid (you should have about ½ cup), and discard the vegetables and bouquet garni.

Sprinkle both sides of the meat with salt and pepper.

Warm the remaining 2 tablespoons olive oil in a large ovenproof sauté pan over high heat. Add the venison and sauté until evenly browned, about 3 to 4 minutes on each side. Immediately place the pan in the oven and cook until the meat is done according to taste, 8 to 9 minutes for medium rare, turning it over at least once while cooking.

Remove the venison from the pan and set it aside on a cutting board to rest.

Discard the fat from the pan and place the pan over high heat. Crush the remaining 1 tablespoon peppercorns and add with the brandy. Deglaze quickly by stirring and scraping all over the sides and bottom of the pan to loosen the browned bits. Add the sherry vinegar and the marinade reduction. Add the veal stock and bring the sauce to a boil. Season with salt and pepper to taste. Swirl in the butter until it is completely melted.

Warm the quince puree in a small saucepan over medium heat.

Slice the venison into ¾-inch-thick slices.

Spread a small bed of quince on each plate and lay 2 or 3 slices of venison on top. Spoon the sauce on top of the meat and serve immediately.

Quinces and cantaloupes at the market in St.-Jean-Pied-de-Port.

MEATS

LAMB

ROASTED LAMB LOIN WITH
GARLIC AND THYME   136

BARBECUED LAMB CHOPS
BASQUAISE   138

LEG OF LAMB "ZIKIRO"   139

LAMB STEW WITH MIXED
NUT PESTO   140

ROLLED LAMB SHOULDER
WITH OLIVE PUREE
AND GROUND ALMOND
POWDER   142

BEEF

BEEF SHORT RIBS WITH
ROASTED BEETS IN RED WINE
SAUCE   144

GRILLED BEEF CROSS RIB
WITH ANCHOVY BUTTER   146

PORK

APPLE CIDER PORK
ROAST   148

BLOOD SAUSAGE WITH
CABBAGE AND APPLE   150

LADIES' RICE   151

HONEY-GLAZED
SPARERIBS   152

VEAL

BRAISED VEAL SWEETBREADS
IN PORT WINE SAUCE   154

VEAL LOIN WITH BAYONNE
HAM AND SHEEP'S MILK
CHEESE   156

VEAL STEW WITH
PEPPERS   159

ROASTED LAMB LOIN WITH GARLIC AND THYME

Arkume Erreta Baratxuri-Xarbotekin

A few years ago, I was invited to cook the main course for the grand dinner of the Napa Valley Wine Auction, an event for nearly 1,800 people. I chose to prepare this lamb loin because a festive Basque meal will always include lamb.

This is a great dish for parties because it can be fully assembled ahead of time and cooks in so short a time. Since caul fat may be difficult to find, I have made it optional. However, I encourage you to make the effort. It adds a subtle flavor to the meat while keeping it very moist and tender. I frequently serve this dish on a bed of Onion and Pepper Confit (page 173) with the garlic scattered around the plate.

SERVES 4

- 2 quarts water
- 16 garlic cloves, peeled
- 4 tablespoons olive oil
- 2 tablespoons finely chopped fresh thyme
- Kosher salt
- Freshly ground white pepper
- 2 pieces caul fat large enough to wrap lamb loins (optional)
- 2 lamb loins (about ¾ pound each), trimmed of fat and silver skin
- ¼ cup dry white wine
- ½ cup Veal Stock (page 228)
- 1 tablespoon unsalted butter
- Onion and Pepper Confit (page 173)
- *Piment d'Espelette* (optional)

Bring 2 quarts of water to a boil. Add the 16 peeled garlic cloves, and continue cooking until the garlic is very tender, 15 to 20 minutes. Rinse the garlic under cold running water for 30 seconds. Set aside.

Preheat the oven to 450 degrees F.

In a mixing bowl, combine 6 cooked garlic cloves with 1 tablespoon olive oil.

Using a fork or wire whisk, mash the ingredients together. Add the thyme and salt and pepper to taste; mix well.

Spread out the 2 pieces of caul fat, if using, and lay a lamb loin in the center of each piece. Rub the garlic and herb puree evenly over both sides of the loins. Neatly wrap the caul fat around the lamb loins and arrange on a baking sheet.

Warm 2 tablespoons olive oil in a large ovenproof sauté pan over high heat. Add the loins and cook just until browned on each side, about 3 minutes. Place the sauté pan in the preheated oven, and cook the meat until medium rare, about 8 minutes.

Warm the remaining 1 tablespoon olive oil in a sauté pan over high heat. Add the 10 remaining garlic cloves and sauté until lightly browned, 2 to 3 minutes. Add the wine and deglaze by stirring and scraping all over the sides and bottom of the pan to loosen the browned bits. Cook until the wine reduces by half. Add the stock and bring to a boil. Swirl in the butter and season with salt and pepper to taste.

Just before the lamb and the garlic sauce are ready, warm the Onion and Pepper Confit over medium-high heat.

Spoon the confit onto the center of a warmed platter or individual plates. Promptly cut the lamb loins into ¾-inch-thick slices and arrange several on or around the confit. Spoon the sauce evenly over the lamb. Dust each plate lightly with *piment d'Espelette.*

BARBECUED LAMB CHOPS BASQUAISE

Arkume Eskualdun

In a country of sheepherders, it is not surprising that the most important meat is lamb. For festivals, whole or quartered lambs are roasted while a wide range of savory lamb stews constitute daily fare. Thick loin lamb chops are one of my favorite cuts. In summer, when it is so easy to cook outdoors, I marinate the chops for a few hours in Basquaise Sauce and then grill them, distilling the taste of the Basque country. You can also sauté the marinated chops over medium-high heat with equal success.

SERVES 4

6 lamb loin chops (5 ounces each), 1½ inches thick

1 cup Basquaise Sauce (page 232)

2 tablespoons brown sugar

Kosher salt

Freshly ground white pepper

Pinch of *piment d'Espelette*

Trim excess fat off the lamb chops.

Place the meat in a shallow baking dish. Rub the meat with Basquaise sauce, brown sugar, salt, pepper, and *piment d'Espelette.*

Cover with plastic wrap, and refrigerate overnight, or for at least for 4 hours, turning the chops over once or twice while marinating.

Preheat a barbecue or grill. Place the chops on the grill and cook until done according to taste, turning once, 4 to 5 minutes a side for medium rare.

Leg of Lamb "Zikiro."

LEG OF LAMB "ZIKIRO"

Arkume Zikiro

All that is left of the witches of Zagarramurdi is a feast every August 15 in the caves where they supposedly danced and held their rituals. A witch-hunt in 1610 resulted in twelve witches and wizards burned at the stake; but forty years later the people of Zagarramurdi, a village close to the French-Spanish border in northern Navarra, were still frightened enough to make a procession to the caves to perform a purging ritual. No witches have been seen since. A feast at the caves commemorates the procession and its successful conclusion. A huge fire is built of a single prostrate tree trunk. Quartered lambs, *zikiro*, are impaled on stakes set in the ground directly in front of the fire. The stakes are turned regularly to allow for even cooking. The lamb fat falls directly onto the ground, not into the fire, so there is no acrid smoke to alter the flavors in the meat.

SERVES 8 TO 10

- ¾ cup olive oil
- ½ cup sherry vinegar
- ⅓ cup chopped fresh thyme
- 1 head of garlic, thinly sliced
- 1 teaspoon *piment d'Espelette*
- 1 tablespoon kosher salt
- 1 tablespoon freshly ground white pepper
- 1 butterflied leg of lamb (about 7 pounds)
- 3 cups water

Preheat the oven to 500 degrees F.

Combine the olive oil, sherry vinegar, thyme, garlic, *piment d'Espelette*, salt, and pepper. Rub the marinade over the meat. Cover tightly and marinate for 2 hours.

Place the lamb on a rack in a roasting pan. Pour the marinade over the lamb, and add 2 cups of water to the bottom of the pan. Cook for 1¼ hours, basting frequently.

Set aside on a cutting board to rest for 20 minutes, covered with aluminum foil.

Drain the fat from the roasting pan and place the pan over medium-high heat. Deglaze with 1 cup of water by stirring and scraping to loosen the browned bits. Bring to a boil and pour into a gravy boat, before spooning over the sliced lamb.

TIP: *At home, a rotisserie works well. Otherwise, you can use a roasting rack as we have done here. Just make sure to baste often for the best results.*

LAMB STEW WITH MIXED NUT PESTO

The Rodriquez-Hernandorena family has turned a majestic old monastery into the serene Remelluri winery in the heart of what locals call the "Basque Mediterranean," the western corner of the Rioja Alavesa. The Pyrenees and Cantabrian Mountains catch the Atlantic winds and rain so that this part of Spanish Basque country, on the southern flanks of the mountains, is both dry and hot. The morning my wife and I arrived for a tour and lunch, everyone was scurrying around the kitchen, apologizing because the house cook for over 30 years, Vittoria, had been called away. Despite the family's concern, the lunch was one of the most memorable meals of my life. The conviviality around the generous table as well as the delicious wines made a superb accompaniment to the lamb with nut sauce. The nut "pesto" we enjoyed that afternoon was made with a mortar and pestle. This method is slower than a food processor, but the result gives the dish a more rustic texture and character.

SERVES 4 TO 6

- 6 tablespoons olive oil
- 4 pounds boneless lamb shoulder, cut into 1-inch cubes
- 1 medium leek, trimmed and cut into ½-inch dice
- 1 medium onion, cut into ½-inch dice
- 1 medium carrot, cut into ½-inch dice
- 4 cups Veal Stock (page 228) or canned low-salt chicken broth
- 1 tablespoon kosher salt
- ¼ teaspoon freshly ground white pepper
- 4 garlic cloves, peeled
- ⅓ cup hazelnuts
- ⅓ cup walnuts
- ⅓ cup almonds
- 2 teaspoons extra-virgin olive oil
- 2 tablespoons unsalted butter
- 2 tablespoons chopped fresh parsley

Warm 2 tablespoons of olive oil in a large, heavy-bottomed saucepan over high heat. Working in two batches, add the lamb and sauté until it begins to brown, 2 to 3 minutes. Transfer the meat to a colander using a slotted spoon. Repeat with 2 more tablespoons olive oil and the remaining lamb.

Add the leek, onion, carrot, and 2 remaining tablespoons olive oil; sauté for 2 to 3 minutes.

Gerald Hirigoyen with Remelluri winery owner Amaia Hernandorena and her family.

Return the meat to the pan. Add the veal stock, salt, and pepper, and bring to a boil. Reduce the heat to a simmer, cover, and cook, stirring occasionally, until the lamb is cooked through and very tender, about 50 minutes. Occasionally skim the top to remove any visible fat.

Using a mortar and pestle, grind the garlic, hazelnuts, walnuts, almonds, and extra-virgin olive oil into a chunky pesto.

Strain the cooking liquid from the lamb into a small saucepan. Transfer the meat to a deep serving platter and cover with aluminum foil to keep warm.

Place the cooking liquid over high heat and cook until reduced by half, occasionally skimming the surface. Add the nut pesto and return to a boil. Reduce the heat and simmer for 5 minutes. Swirl in the butter until melted. Season with salt and pepper to taste.

Pour the sauce over the lamb, and garnish with the parsley.

ROLLED LAMB SHOULDER WITH OLIVE PUREE AND GROUND ALMOND POWDER

Arkume Espalda Oliba eta Arbendelekin

Each year shortly after Easter, Basque shepherds lead their flocks into the high mountain meadows to graze; they may not return before October. The shepherds milk their sheep twice a day and make their famous mountain cheeses. By the end of summer, a steady stream of cars heads into the mountains in search of *kayolas* (sheepherders' shacks), where one can purchase rounds of the handmade cheeses. This is one of the few times sheepherders are likely to see company other than in June, just before the summer's heat, when the sheep are shorn and people come in search of the wool. Easter lamb, stuffed with olives and almonds, is traditionally served right before the sheepherders depart for the summer.

SERVES 4 TO 6

5 pounds boned lamb shoulder, fat trimmed

1 tablespoon kosher salt

Freshly ground white pepper

1 teaspoon *piment d'Espelette*

½ cup tapenade (see Tip)

½ cup Ground Almond Powder (page 235)

String

½ cup olive oil

1 medium onion, quartered

1 cup peeled garlic cloves

3 cups dry white wine

1 cup Vegetable Stock (page 229) or canned vegetable broth

Preheat the oven to 425 degrees F.

Lay the shoulder as flat as possible, slicing the meat open like an envelope where necessary to achieve a somewhat "square" surface. Sprinkle the side facing up with 1 tablespoon kosher salt, at least 30 turns of a pepper mill, and the *piment d'Espelette*. Spread the tapenade evenly over the same side and scatter the ground almond powder on top. Roll the lamb up tightly and secure with kitchen string in several places. Sprinkle salt and pepper liberally all over the roll.

Warm the olive oil in a roasting pan over high heat. Add the rolled meat and brown it all over, about 8 minutes. Add the onion and garlic to the pan and immediately place it in the oven.

Cook for 15 minutes, turn the lamb over, and add the white wine.

Cook for 1 hour, basting the meat every 15 minutes.

Add the vegetable stock, and cook for 15 minutes longer.

Transfer the roast to a cutting board, and cover with aluminum foil to keep warm. Let it rest for 20 minutes before slicing.

Strain the pan juices from the roasting pan through a sieve into a small saucepan. Discard the vegetables.

Heat the pan juices over medium-high heat, skimming any visible fat. Season with salt and pepper to taste.

Slice the lamb and arrange on a platter. Drizzle the juice around the meat.

TIP: *Tapenade is olive paste flavored with herbs and anchovies. It is available in specialty food shops, or you can make your own by processing 1 cup pitted, oil-cured black olives, 1½ tablespoons capers, 6 to 8 anchovies, 1 teaspoon thyme leaves, salt to taste, and 2 teaspoons extra-virgin olive oil. The tapenade is then forced through a fine-mesh strainer and is ready to use.*

BEEF SHORT RIBS WITH ROASTED BEETS IN RED WINE SAUCE

Idi Kostak eta Erremolatxa Arnoa Gorrian

Aficionados of bullfights often gather to discuss the day's events around a bubbling pot of stew made from bull meat. Bullfights take place in the summer, but I would recommend making this dish in winter, when long-simmered dishes taste their best.

Beef short ribs, marinated overnight with vegetables, wine, herbs, and seasonings, are very flavorful and tender when cooked by this method. I have used a few beets here, but you can easily substitute other winter vegetables such as parsnips, turnips, or potatoes.

SERVES 4 OR 5

ROASTED BEETS

2 medium red or golden beets

About 3 tablespoons olive oil

Kosher salt

Freshly ground white pepper

SHORT RIBS

5 pounds beef short ribs

2 cups coarsely chopped carrots

1½ cups coarsely chopped celery

1 cup coarsely chopped onion

6 garlic cloves, peeled and crushed

1 bouquet garni

1 tablespoon juniper berries

2 tablespoons black peppercorns

4 cups dry red wine

⅔ cup plus 1 teaspoon olive oil

5 cups Veal Stock (page 228) or beef stock

Kosher salt

Freshly ground white pepper

¼ cup (½ stick) unsalted butter

TO MAKE THE ROASTED BEETS

Preheat the oven to 375 degrees F.

Lay the beets on a sheet pan lined with aluminum foil. Drizzle 2 tablespoons olive oil over the beets, wrap them in the foil, and roast in the oven until tender, 1¾ to 2 hours.

Cool the beets until you can handle them. Peel them and cut them into quarters. Drizzle with olive oil to taste and sprinkle with salt and pepper.

TO MAKE THE RIBS

In a large nonaluminum bowl, combine short ribs, carrots, celery, onion, garlic cloves, bouquet garni, juniper berries, black peppercorns, red wine, and ⅓ cup olive oil, making sure that the meat is completely submerged in the marinade. Cover and refrigerate overnight.

Drain the meat and vegetables in a colander suspended over a bowl, capturing the liquid marinade. Separate the meat from the vegetables and bouquet garni, and set them aside.

Villagers in the town of Sare.

Warm ⅓ cup olive oil in a large sauté pan over high heat. Add the short ribs and brown them on each side, 2 to 3 minutes. Transfer the ribs back to the colander to drain excess fat from the meat.

To the same pan, add the reserved vegetables and the remaining 1 teaspoon of olive oil. Sauté over medium-high heat until they begin to brown, about 3 to 4 minutes.

Combine the reserved marinade, short ribs, and bouquet garni in a large saucepan. Bring to a boil. When the vegetables are browned, add them to the saucepan along with the veal stock and bring to a boil. Reduce heat and let simmer, uncovered, until the meat is cooked through and very tender, 1 to 1½ hours.

TO ASSEMBLE

Strain the cooking liquid from the short ribs into a shallow saucepan. Set the meat aside and discard the vegetables and the bouquet garni.

Bring the sauce to a boil, skimming off any visible fat. Add the roasted beets and season with salt and pepper to taste. Add the butter and stir until it has completely melted into the sauce.

Place the short ribs and beets on a large serving platter and pour the sauce on top.

GRILLED BEEF CROSS RIB WITH ANCHOVY BUTTER

Idi Kostak Antxozko Gurinarekin

Good beef is more popular in the Basque country than it used to be but still falls behind lamb, pork, and veal. A simple grilled steak with perhaps a sprinkling of *piment d'Espelette* is a staple menu item at the *cidreries*, the cider-tasting restaurants. This recipe is very easy, the flavor coming from the grill and the flavored butter. You can also treat steaks such as porterhouse or sirloin in the same manner.

SERVES 2 OR 3

1 ounce salted anchovy fillets, rinsed and finely diced

4 tablespoons unsalted butter

½ teaspoon minced fresh rosemary

¼ teaspoon *piment d'Espelette*

2 pounds beef cross rib (in one piece)

1 tablespoon olive oil

Kosher salt

Freshly ground white pepper

Preheat a barbecue or grill.

In a mortar or small bowl, pound the anchovies into a paste. Add the butter, rosemary, and *piment d'Espelette*. Combine well and set aside.

Brush the meat with the olive oil and season generously with salt and pepper. Place the meat on the grill, turning occasionally until cooked according to taste, about 6 minutes for rare, 8 minutes for medium, and 10 minutes for well done.

Place the meat on a serving platter and let it rest for 5 minutes before slicing. Spoon the anchovy butter on top of the meat.

APPLE CIDER PORK ROAST

Txerrikia Sagardoan

SERVES 4

One 8-bone center rib roast
  of pork, backbone removed

2 teaspoons kosher salt

Freshly ground white pepper

½ cup olive oil

1 medium onion, coarsely
  chopped

2 large green apples,
  quartered

2 large celery stalks, coarsely
  chopped

1 cup fermented apple cider

2 cups Vegetable Stock (page
  229)

½ cup brown sugar

Fall is the traditional pig butchering season and it is also the season of apples, a primary crop used mainly to make a dry, slightly pétillant cider. The combination of pork, apples, and cider gives this dish an aromatic, sweet, and savory flavor. In the old days tavern keepers and restaurateurs would visit *cidreries* (cider producers, usually a farmer with a large orchard) to taste the various barrels in order to decide which ones to buy. Eventually, the tasting ritual evolved into a democratic affair. *Cidreries* open their doors in January when the new cider has just finished fermenting. Tasting the fresh cider has become a favorite Basque excuse for a party. In May most of the *cidreries* close and the cider is bottled.

To minimize the side effects of tasting, the *cidreries* began offering food, usually cooked by the farmer's wife. Large barbecues were set up and grilled beef and fish were served in addition to omelets, salt cod, and cheese plates. The food has become so well known that now people go to *cidreries* specifically to eat. Everyone sits on benches at long communal tables. Every so often a signal is given and those who wish to taste the cider go into a room full of large wooden fermentation casks. The faucet on a cask is turned and out spouts an arc of pale cider. The trick is to get in line to fill your glass from the stream and move on without spilling any or getting wet yourself. Then the tasters return to the tables to eat and talk some more, then more tasting, more talking, more tasting, more eating.

Pierre Oteiza Charcuterie in Les Aldudes.

Preheat the oven to 450 degrees F.

If your butcher has not already done so, trim the meat between the rib bones and set aside the trimmings. Sprinkle salt and pepper all over the pork.

Put the olive oil in a roasting pan. Place the meat, rib side down, in the pan. Scatter the onion, apples, celery, and meat trimmings around the roast.

Place the roast in the oven to cook for 15 minutes.

Turn and cook the roast for another 15 minutes. Then add the cider, vegetable stock, and brown sugar to the pan.

Cook for 40 to 45 minutes, until the meat is cooked to an internal temperature of 150 to 155 degrees F., basting it approximately every 15 minutes.

Transfer the meat to a cutting board, cover with aluminum foil to keep warm, and let it rest for 10 to 15 minutes.

Strain the liquid from the roasting pan through a fine-mesh sieve into a small saucepan, and discard the vegetables. Season with salt and pepper to taste and bring to a boil.

Carve the roast by cutting between the bones. Arrange the chops on a large platter and spoon the apple cider *jus* on top of the meat.

BLOOD SAUSAGE WITH CABBAGE AND APPLE

Odolgia Aza eta Sagarrekin

Each November the townspeople of Biriatou in Labourd province celebrate the Feast of Saint Martin, the patron saint of geese, wine, and drunkards. The traditional dish of the festival is *tripotx*, blood sausage made from lamb or tripe instead of the usual pork, and cooked with cabbage. Blood sausage is still widely made in Basque country *caserios* (farmhouses), but for most Americans the ingredients are esoteric as well as hard to find. My friend and expert sausage maker, Henri Lapuyade of Marcel & Henri, makes one of the best commercial versions of this rich, savory sausage. It can be found in upscale supermarkets and specialty food shops.

Preheat broiler.

Warm ⅓ cup olive oil in a large sauté pan over medium-high heat. Add the bacon, cabbage, 1 teaspoon salt, and ½ teaspoon ground pepper. Sauté for 5 to 6 minutes, until thoroughly wilted. Transfer the cabbage to an earthenware casserole and set aside.

Using the same pan, sauté the julienned apple with the 1 remaining tablespoon olive oil and ¼ teaspoon *piment d'Espelette* over high heat for 1 minute. Then scatter the apple on top of the cabbage.

Slice the sausage in ⅓-inch-thick pieces and remove the casing from each slice. Then fan the sausage in a barely overlapping spiral formation on top of the apple and cabbage. Scatter the butter and bread crumbs on top of the sausage and place under the broiler until the surface is nicely browned, 7 to 8 minutes.

TIP: *Remember to remove the tough casing after slicing the sausage. (If you remove it earlier, the sausage may fall apart.)*

SERVES 4

⅓ cup plus 1 tablespoon olive oil

2 ounces slab bacon

1 medium head of cabbage, cored and finely sliced

1 teaspoon kosher salt

½ teaspoon freshly ground white pepper

1 medium green apple, cored, peeled, and finely julienned

¼ teaspoon *piment d'Espelette* (optional)

1 pound blood sausage

2 tablespoons fine bread crumbs

4 tablespoons (½ stick) unsalted butter, broken into small pieces

LADIES' RICE

I think of this dish from the French Basque provinces as "paella for the poor" because it is a tasty, generous main dish that does not require expensive ingredients. The simple recipe I give here can become the base for endless variations by adding such ingredients as olives, chicken, bacon, seafood, and seasonal produce including tomatoes, peas, fava beans, and artichokes. Cook them separately, then add to the dish for the last few minutes of cooking. *Gaxucha*, as this dish is nicknamed, is the Basque word for the woman's name Grace, so perhaps the dish is named after the woman who created it. Over the years, however, it has somehow become known as Ladies' Rice or Gracious Rice, possibly because the French word *"Gracieuse"* is also a woman's name. Spelled with a lowercase "g," however, the same word means gracious.

SERVES 4 TO 6

¾ cup finely diced onion

⅓ cup finely diced red bell peppers

⅓ cup finely diced Anaheim chiles

½ pound chorizo, thinly sliced

½ cup olive oil

2 cups long-grain rice

3¾ cups water

Kosher salt

Freshly ground white pepper

Pinch of *piment d'Espelette*

Preheat the oven to 450 degrees F.

Sauté the onion, red bell peppers, Anaheim chiles, and chorizo with the olive oil in a large ovenproof casserole over medium heat until the vegetables begin to brown, about 4 minutes.

Stir in the rice and water, cover, and place in the oven until tender, 20 to 25 minutes. Season with salt, pepper, and *piment d'Espelette* to taste.

HONEY-GLAZED SPARERIBS

Txerriki Kostak Eztiarekin

It used to be that during Lent, monks were allowed to eat only what was fished from the river running past the monastery. Legend has it that a few quick-witted monks used to sneak upstream and toss a few pigs into the water. Their accomplices would catch them as they floated past the monastery. Pork, from the head to the tail, has historically been consumed in large amounts throughout the Basque country. In the French provinces, much of the pork was made into confit. As a boy, I couldn't wait until I would be allowed to pull a nice rack of ribs out of the confit crock. Then the ribs were grilled until they were crispy and hot. This far simpler preparation produces finger-licking results.

SERVES 3 OR 4

3½ to 4 pounds pork
  spareribs

Kosher salt

¾ cup honey

1 teaspoon *piment d'Espelette*

2 teaspoons sherry vinegar

3 garlic cloves, minced

1 tablespoon black
  peppercorns, well crushed

1 tablespoon coriander seeds,
  well crushed

Preheat the oven to 375 degrees F.

Line a large sheet pan with aluminum foil and lay the rack of ribs on top.

Season both sides of the meat with salt.

To prepare the glaze, combine the honey, *piment d'Espelette*, sherry vinegar, garlic, black peppercorns, and coriander seeds in a small bowl; mix together well.

Slather the glaze evenly over both sides of the meat and place the ribs in the oven to cook for 45 minutes, basting continuously. Then turn the slab over and increase the heat to 425 degrees F. Cook for another 30 minutes, basting once or twice more, until the meat is cooked through and the glaze is dark brown.

BRAISED VEAL SWEETBREADS IN PORT WINE SAUCE

Muna Erretak Portotan

SERVES 4 TO 6 AS AN APPETIZER OR 3 OR 4 AS A MAIN COURSE

2½ pounds veal sweetbreads

4 tablespoons (½ stick) unsalted butter

2 small celery ribs, finely diced

1 small onion, finely diced

1 small carrot, finely diced

3 garlic cloves, finely sliced

1 cup port wine

1 teaspoon kosher salt

¼ teaspoon freshly ground white pepper

1 bouquet garni

1 cup Veal Stock (page 228)

When an animal is butchered in Basque country, nothing goes to waste. Consequently, we have many dishes for sweetbreads, kidneys, and tripe. When I first came to California in 1980, few Basque restaurants remained in San Francisco, but the family-style Basque Hotel on Broadway was still very busy. Groups sat together at long tables and, for very reasonable prices, enjoyed course after course of good food. As was common in this style of restaurant, a daily menu was served and was repeated each week. I loved to go for the veal sweetbreads. They have a rich, subtle, refined flavor that has converted many of my restaurants' customers. And because they are rich, they can be served as an appetizer as well as a main course.

Soak the sweetbreads in water for 2 hours, changing the water two or three times.

Place the sweetbreads in a large saucepan. Cover generously with water and bring to a boil. Remove from the heat, drain, and rinse the sweetbreads under cold running water. Remove any excess fat, gristle, and membranes. Set aside.

Preheat the oven to 475 degrees F.

In the same saucepan, warm 3 tablespoons of butter over medium-high heat. Add the celery, onion, carrot, and garlic. Sauté until the vegetables begin to brown and soften, about 5 minutes. Add the sweetbreads, port, salt, pepper, and bouquet garni.

Cover the pan and put it in the oven for 5 minutes. Turn the sweetbreads over and continue to cook for another 5 minutes. Add the veal stock and cook until the sweetbreads have lost much of their elasticity when pressure is applied, about 6 minutes longer.

View from Domaine Brana's Irouleguy vineyards.

Transfer the sweetbreads to a serving platter. Cover with aluminum foil to keep warm and set aside.

Strain the sauce away from the vegetables into a small saucepan and discard the vegetables. Bring the sauce to a boil, reduce the heat to medium, and skim any visible fat. Season with salt and pepper to taste. Swirl the 1 remaining tablespoon of butter into the sauce until completely melted. Place the sweetbreads on a serving platter and pour the sauce on top.

VEAL LOIN WITH BAYONNE HAM AND SHEEP'S MILK CHEESE

Txahalkiko Solomo Baionako Xingar eta Ardi-Gasnarekin

This is a dish for any special occasion. It is beautiful and delicious, and once it is assembled, there is very little to do. Veal, a popular meat in the Basque country, tends to dry out during cooking. This method—the meat is rolled up with Bayonne ham and cheese—helps to keep it moist. Serve the dish with Creamy Mashed Potatoes (page 169) or Green Peas with Bayonne Ham (page 174).

SERVES 6

2 pounds veal loin, trimmed

Kosher salt

Freshly ground white pepper

8 ounces semisoft sheep's milk cheese

10 to 12 thin slices of Bayonne ham or prosciutto (about 10 ounces)

String

½ cup olive oil

1 small celery root, peeled and diced

1 small carrot, diced

1 small onion, diced

10 garlic cloves

1 tablespoon black peppercorns

3 sprigs fresh thyme

1 cup dry white wine

1 cup Veal Stock (page 228)

Preheat the oven to 450 degrees F.

Using a sharp knife, butterfly the veal lengthwise down the center, and pull open the flaps of meat so that it may be seasoned and stuffed. Season the meat with salt and pepper.

Distribute the cheese lengthwise down the center of the veal. Close the meat back up around the cheese, squeezing it shut as tightly as possible. Set aside.

Arrange the ham on a flat work surface so that each slice overlaps the next. When all of the slices are spread out, they should extend the same length as the loin. Lay the loin, centered horizontally, on top of the ham. Carefully wrap the slices up around the veal, and secure them with string tied strategically in several places to keep the ham in place during cooking.

Combine the olive oil, celery root, carrot, onion, garlic, black peppercorns, and thyme in a roasting pan. Place the veal in the center of the pan, and put in the oven to roast for 15 minutes.

Turn the loin over, add the white wine and veal stock, and continue roasting just until firm, about 15 minutes longer.

(continued)

Transfer the meat to a cutting board. Cover with aluminum foil and let rest for at least 15 minutes.

Strain the remaining contents of the roasting pan through a sieve into a small saucepan, and bring to a boil, skimming off any visible fat and reducing the liquid somewhat.

Cut the veal into ½-inch-thick slices. Arrange the meat on a warmed serving platter or individual plates. Spoon the pan juices on top.

The famous Hotel Euzkadi in Espelette.

VEAL STEW WITH PEPPERS

Ezpeletako Axoa

This dish is a specialty of Espelette in Labourd province, where the best *axoa* can be found at the Hotel Euzkadi, in the center of the village. André Darraïdou, owner and chef of the hotel, is also the mayor of Espelette, and founder, in 1967, of the *piment d'Espelette* festival. Today thousands of people come from all over Europe to join in the celebration. *Axoa* includes whole peppers as well as a big pinch of *piment d'Espelette*, affectionately known as "red gold." It is normally prepared on market day and is made with veal or beef, but a few renegades have been known to make it with chicken. It is usually served on a large platter with a green salad and some Fried Garlic Potatoes (page 168). A glass of red Irouleguy wine is a great partner for this dish.

SERVES 4

⅓ cup Rendered Duck Fat (page 231) or olive oil

1 small onion, thinly sliced

4 Anaheim chiles, seeded and finely julienned

1 medium red bell pepper, cored and finely julienned

4 garlic cloves, crushed

1½ pounds boneless veal leg or shoulder, cut in 1-inch-thick strips

1 teaspoon kosher salt

⅛ teaspoon freshly ground white pepper

1 bouquet garni

1 cup dry white wine

In a large casserole over medium-high heat, combine the duck fat, onion, chiles, red bell pepper, and garlic. Sauté for 2 minutes.

Add the veal, salt, pepper, bouquet garni, and white wine and bring to a boil. Simmer until the meat is done, about 45 minutes.

Piquillo. Extra
3 Kilos. 450

toma
PERA

Piquillo
LODE

VEGETABLES AND ACCOMPANIMENTS

BEET LEAF FRITTERS

Beltaraba Ostozko Kruspetak

I tasted these fritters as part of a wonderful lunch prepared by the owners of the Remelluri winery in the Rioja Alavesa. Any of the slightly bitter leafy greens, including chard, spinach, kale, and beet greens, would work for these fritters. I prefer beet greens because they are the sweetest-tasting and most quickly cooked. Interestingly enough, beets used to be grown especially for their greens while the beets themselves were thrown out. Serve the fritters as a side dish with fish or lamb, as we enjoyed them at Remelluri, or even as a snack.

SERVES 4 TO 6

- 1 cup flour
- Pinch of kosher salt
- Pinch of freshly ground white pepper
- 2 tablespoons (¼ stick) unsalted butter, melted
- 1 cup cold water
- ½ teaspoon baking soda
- 1 pound beet leaves or Swiss chard, well washed
- 1 quart vegetable oil
- Freshly ground black pepper

Combine the flour, salt, pepper, butter, water, and baking soda in a large mixing bowl. Mix well and set aside for 1 hour.

Fill a large saucepan half full of water and bring to a boil.

Pull the leaves lengthwise off their spines, discard the spines, and blanch the leaves in the boiling water for 30 seconds. Drain and set aside. Squeeze the leaves to remove all of the remaining water, then spread the leaves out onto a towel to dry further.

Divide the leaves into 16 piles, then squeeze each pile into a golf-ball-sized round.

Heat the vegetable oil in a deep fryer or heavy-bottomed saucepan. When the oil is about 375 degrees F., dip 2 or 3 beet leaf balls into the batter, then into the oil to fry until the batter is golden brown and crispy and the fritters are heated through, 1 to 2 minutes. Drain the fritters on a paper towels. Repeat with the remaining beet leaf balls. Garnish with a few turns of freshly ground black pepper. Serve immediately.

SPINACH

Spinach is most often served in the Basque country blanched, squeezed dry, then sautéed in butter or other fat. I prefer the milder, fresher, sweeter taste of this method, where the leaves just wilt and retain their vibrant color. You do need a good amount of fat to coat the leaves but most of it will be drained off before serving.

SERVES 4

⅓ cup olive oil

3 tablespoons unsalted butter

1½ pounds spinach leaves, stems removed

1 tablespoon kosher salt

¼ teaspoon freshly ground white pepper

¼ cup vegetable stock (page 229) or water

Warm olive oil and butter in a very large casserole over medium-high heat until hot.

Add half of the spinach and season with salt and pepper. Add the remaining spinach and season again. Add the vegetable stock. Cook for 1 minute, stir for a few seconds, then cover, and continue to cook just until wilted and still bright green, 2 to 3 minutes.

Drain and serve immediately.

ZUCCHINI À LA MINUTE

Kuiatxoak

Like just about everywhere in the world where vegetables are grown, Basque gardens and markets overflow with zucchini during the summer season. This is a very easily prepared recipe that gives maximum impact. Leave the skin on for color and mix yellow and green zucchini for added interest. The dish tastes best if the zucchini remain a little crunchy. Serve it warm as a side dish or cold as a salad, adding a splash of sherry or champagne vinegar.

SERVES 4 TO 6 AS A SIDE DISH, 4 AS A SALAD

3½ pounds zucchini

⅓ cup olive oil

1 cup loosely packed basil leaves

1 teaspoon kosher salt

1 teaspoon freshly ground white pepper

⅛ teaspoon *piment d'Espelette* (optional)

Using a mandoline or sharp knife, finely julienne the zucchini lengthwise up to the core. Discard the core.

Warm ⅓ cup olive oil in a large casserole over high heat. When the oil is hot, add the zucchini and basil. Add salt, pepper, and *piment d'Espelette,* if using. Stir frequently until zucchini starts to soften, about 2 minutes. Season with salt and pepper to taste.

SAUTÉED SALSIFY

Terebuza

When I was less than ten years old, I decided I didn't like salsify, even though I had never tasted it. One night my father told me I was not to leave the table until I had finished my salsify. Being as stubborn as all Basques, I fell asleep at the table and never touched a bite. Now I am a huge fan of this vegetable. Salsify is a root with a shape like a carrot or parsnip. Its season is late fall and winter, and its taste is somewhere between asparagus and artichoke.

SERVES 4 TO 6

½ lemon

2 pounds salsify

6 tablespoons (¾ stick) unsalted butter

3 tablespoons chopped fresh parsley

Kosher salt

Freshly ground white pepper

To make a lemon bath, squeeze the lemon into a large bowl of water; set aside.

Peel the salsify stalks individually. Cut stalks into 2½-inch pieces and drop them into the lemon bath as you go. This will keep the salsify from discoloring.

Fill a large pot three-quarters full of water and bring to a boil.

Drain the salsify, and add it to the boiling water. Cover and boil until tender, about 12 minutes. Drain and set aside. In the same pot, melt the butter over medium-high heat. Add the salsify and sauté until golden, 4 to 5 minutes. Toss with the parsley, and season with salt and pepper to taste.

NEW POTATO AND ROMANO BEAN RAGOUT

Lursagar Berri eta Babarrun Saltsa

Romano beans—wide, flat, usually green beans—are very popular in and around San Sebastián where they are often cooked with a little ham or chorizo. Romano beans can be green and sometimes yellow but are always wide and flat. They are available in the United States throughout the summer, and some are grown in Mexico and imported in the winter. The best sources may be farmers' markets and specialty produce markets. Romanos remain longer on the vine to ripen and thus have a short shelf life. This ragout makes a great side dish for roast chicken or a lamb stew such as Lamb Stew with Mixed Nut Pesto (page 140). If you choose to add some Bayonne ham or chorizo, dice it small and add it to the sauté pan with the beans and potatoes. With the addition of meat, the dish could be served as an appetizer or even as supper with a piece of cheese and a loaf of crusty bread.

SERVES 4

2 pounds green Romano beans, trimmed

1 pound small Yukon Gold potatoes, peeled and cut in half

¼ cup olive oil

1 small onion, finely diced

2 small garlic cloves, thinly sliced

Pinch of kosher salt

Freshly ground white pepper

2 tablespoons (¼ stick) unsalted butter

3 tablespoons snipped fresh chives

Bring a large pot of salted water to a boil. Add the beans, and return to a boil. Cook, uncovered, for 4 to 5 minutes. Add the potatoes, return to a boil, and cook until the potatoes are cooked through, about 9 or 10 minutes longer.

Warm the olive oil in a large sauté pan over medium heat. Add the onion and garlic and sweat until they are soft and translucent.

Strain the beans and potatoes over a bowl, reserving ¼ cup of the cooking liquid.

Add the beans and potatoes to the sauté pan. Season with salt and pepper to taste. Add the butter, chopped chives, and ¼ cup reserved cooking liquid. Stir everything together, and continue to sauté until the flavors are well combined and the vegetables are hot, about 3 minutes.

FRIED GARLIC POTATOES

Lursagarrak Baratxuriarekin

In my opinion, nothing beats a heaping pile of potatoes fried in duck fat with lots of garlic. Serve them with Roasted Chicken "Irouleguy" (page 118), with chicken roasted with butter and red wine, or next to your breakfast eggs, a steak, or indeed anything at all.

SERVES 4

⅔ cup Rendered Duck Fat (page 231) or olive oil

2 pounds Yukon Gold potatoes, peeled and cut into 1-inch cubes

10 garlic cloves, very thinly sliced

3 tablespoons chopped fresh parsley

1 teaspoon kosher salt

Freshly ground white pepper

Warm the duck fat (or olive oil) in a large sauté pan over medium heat. Add the potatoes and sauté until they start to soften, 6 or 7 minutes.

Add the garlic and continue to sauté until the potatoes are tender and the garlic is browned, about 9 minutes longer.

Drain the excess fat, and transfer the potatoes to a serving bowl. Garnish the potatoes with the parsley, salt, and pepper. Toss gently and serve immediately.

TIP: *I like to sauté the potatoes starting from their raw state. However, you can also cook the potatoes in boiling salted water until just barely tender, then drain well and sauté until browned. Add the garlic for the last few minutes of cooking to make sure it gets just golden brown and does not burn.*

CREAMY MASHED POTATOES

Any country that grows and eats potatoes must love mashed potatoes! Spanish Basque cooks tend to make almost soupy mashed potatoes. I reflect my French background and much prefer a smooth, thick (but not dense!) potato puree.

SERVES 4 TO 6

2 pounds russet potatoes, peeled and coarsely chopped

Kosher salt

6 tablespoons (¾ stick) unsalted butter, cut into small pieces

1¼ cups hot milk

Freshly ground white pepper

Preheat the oven to 400 degrees F.

Place the potatoes and a pinch of salt in a large saucepan with water to cover. Bring to a boil, cover, and cook until the potatoes are soft and tender, about 25 minutes.

Spread the potatoes on a sheet pan and place in the oven to "dry" for 3 to 4 minutes.

Pass the potatoes through a ricer or strainer into a large pot. Scatter the butter on top of the potatoes and slowly stir in the hot milk, a little at a time, incorporating it fully before adding more. Adjust the consistency by adding more or less milk if desired. Season with salt and pepper to taste.

TIP: *If you like smooth mashed potatoes, it is well worth investing in a potato ricer or vegetable mill. Electric mixers, no matter how careful the cook, give potatoes an elastic consistency. Adjust the amount of milk, up or down, to suit your preference for thick or thinner potatoes. For the most flavor, use whole milk.*

POTATOES RIOJANAS

Lursagar Gorri Saltsa

The fortified town of Laguardia sits alone and high on its plateau looking exactly like the proverbial "castle in Spain." Surrounded by the vineyards of Rioja in the province of Alava, the town—or more truthfully, the cellars of the town—houses the local wineries. So undercut are the streets by the wineries that no trucks or heavy cars are allowed to pass above the bodegas. It was here that my wife and I found a superb little restaurant attached to the bodega Mayor de Migueloa. Our favorite dish was a plate of steaming potatoes cooked in the "house red." It is a typical preparation of the Rioja Alavesa region, so I recommend a good red wine from Rioja for making this dish: a little for the pot and a little for your glass!

SERVES 4 TO 6

⅓ cup olive oil

1 small onion, finely sliced

3 garlic cloves, finely sliced

2 pounds Yukon Gold
potatoes, halved

1 small sprig rosemary

2 cups dry red wine

Kosher salt

Freshly ground white pepper

3 tablespoons unsalted butter

¼ to ½ cup water, if needed

Warm the olive oil in a large, deep saucepan over medium-high heat. Add the onion and garlic, and sauté for 2 to 3 minutes. Add the potatoes, rosemary, red wine, and salt and pepper to taste. Bring to a boil and simmer, stirring occasionally, for 40 minutes. If the liquid evaporates before 40 minutes, you can add a little water (¼ to ½ cup).

Once the potatoes are cooked and tender, stir in the butter. Set the potatoes aside for 5 or 6 minutes before serving.

Opposite page, clockwise
from top left:
Sautéed Salsify (page 166);
Potatoes Riojanas,
Fava Bean Gratin (page 175).

SPANISH WHITE RICE

Arroza Txuri

The rice used for many Spanish dishes, especially paella, is a medium-grain rice with a higher starch content than long-grain rice. If you prefer more separate grains than the risotto-like texture this method yields, rinse the rice under running water before cooking to remove some of the starch. Serve the rice with fish, poultry, and meat dishes such as Stuffed Squid in Ink Sauce (page 80) and Poulet Basquaise (page 120).

SERVES 4 TO 6

6 cups water

1 tablespoon kosher salt

2 cups medium-grain white rice

Unsalted butter (to taste)

Kosher salt

Freshly ground white pepper

Bring the water and salt to a boil.

Add the rice, return to a boil, and reduce the heat to a simmer until the rice is cooked through, about 15 minutes.

Drain excess water. Stir in butter and season with salt and pepper to taste.

SWEETS

CAKES AND TARTS

ALMOND MERINGUE AND
BUTTER CREAM CAKE   182

CORNMEAL CAKE WITH
WARM BERRIES   184

GÂTEAU BASQUE   186

APPLE AND QUINCE TART
189

QUINCE AND GOAT CHEESE
LAYER CAKE WITH CANDIED
PINE NUTS   190

CHOCOLATE

CHOCOLATE ROCKS   192

BERET BASQUE AU
CHOCOLAT   194

BAKED CHOCOLATE CAKE   196

CHOCOLATE TRUFFLES WITH
BRANDY   197

COOKIES AND PASTRIES

MERINGUE MAKILAS   198

ALMOND MACAROONS   200

BLUEBERRY BAYONNAIS   201

ORANGE BLOSSOM
BEIGNETS   202

BASQUE BRIOCHE   204

PASTRY FRITTERS   205

CUSTARDS AND CREAMS

CRÈME CARAMEL   207

CHESTNUT AND CARAMEL
CUSTARD   208

FRIED CREAM SQUARES   209

RICE PUDDING WITH
DRIED APRICOTS   210

GOAT'S MILK CUSTARD WITH
CARAMELIZED FIGS AND
HONEY   212

WALNUT CREAM   213

FRUITS AND CHEESES

CHERRIES IN RED WINE
SOUP   214

WALNUT AND SHEEP'S MILK
CHEESE GRATIN   216

FRUIT AND CHEESE
PLATTER   217

ICE CREAMS, SORBETS, AND PARFAITS

HONEY ICE CREAM   218

IZARRA ICE CREAM   219

GREEN APPLE SORBET   221

POIRE WILLIAM SORBET   222

PATXARAN SORBET   223

TURRON PARFAIT   224

ALMOND MERINGUE AND BUTTER CREAM CAKE

Arbendel Tartaxoa

Butter cream is one of the first things I learned to make as a pastry apprentice. I have loved it and licked my fingers whenever I've made it since. This cake is a staple of fine pastry shops throughout France but is even better when made at home. It may look fussy on the page but will more than reward your efforts. It is a dazzling and practical party dessert because it can be completed—even the cutting of portions!—well ahead of time. Serve the cake alone, drizzled with a seasonal fruit puree, or with a few berries on the side of each plate.

SERVES 6

ALMOND MERINGUE

Melted unsalted butter for brushing the sheet pans

1 cup plus 2 tablespoons Ground Almond Powder (page 235)

1 cup plus 2 tablespoons powdered sugar

2 tablespoons flour

6 egg whites

2 tablespoons sugar

⅓ cup sliced almonds

BUTTER CREAM

1 cup sugar

¼ cup water

6 egg yolks

Seeds from 1 vanilla bean

½ pound (2 sticks) plus 1 tablespoon unsalted butter, at room temperature

Confectioners' sugar for sprinkling

Preheat the oven to 300 degrees F.

To make the meringues, line 2 sheet pans with parchment paper and brush them with melted butter. Using the dull side of a knife tip, draw three 7-inch circles in the melted butter on the parchment paper.

Combine the almond powder, powdered sugar, and flour in a large bowl, using a wire whisk, until evenly incorporated; set aside.

In the work bowl of a standing mixer fitted with the whisk attachment, beat the egg whites into soft peaks. Add the sugar and continue beating until the egg whites reach the hard-peak stage. Fold the dry ingredients into the egg whites and stop as soon as they are combined. You do not want to overwork the batter.

Scoop the batter into a large pastry bag fitted with a ¼-inch round tip or a plastic bag with a corner snipped off, and pipe the batter into the three circles drawn on the prepared sheet pans. Begin in the center and use a tight spiral motion to form the circles. Scatter the sliced almonds evenly over the top of the circles.

Put both of the sheet pans into the oven, and bake until the meringues are golden, puffed, and firm to the touch, about 40 to 45 minutes. Transfer the meringues to a cooling rack to cool completely.

To make the butter cream, combine the sugar and water in a small saucepan over high heat. Bring the ingredients to a boil, stirring occasionally to dissolve the sugar.

In the work bowl of a standing mixer fitted with the whisk attachment, combine the egg yolks and the vanilla bean seeds.

As soon as the syrup reaches "hard ball" stage (about 255 degrees F. on a candy thermometer), remove it from the heat. With the mixer on high speed, pour the sugar syrup directly into the egg yolks and continue to beat on high speed until the ingredients cool sufficiently to incorporate the butter without risk of melting it, 6 to 8 minutes. Scrape down the sides of the bowl as needed. The texture of the butter cream needs to be smooth and silky, but not too thin, or it won't have enough body to support the cake.

Beat in the butter just until evenly combined, about 1 minute.

To assemble the cake, place one of the meringues in the center of a serving platter, and pipe or spoon half of the butter cream evenly on top. Place a second meringue on top of the butter cream. Repeat with the remaining half of the butter cream, and finish with the last meringue.

For best results, place the cake in the refrigerator to set for 1 to 2 hours. Once it has set, slice it into 6 pieces using a serrated knife in a sawing motion. Place the pieces on individual serving plates and set aside until the butter cream reaches room temperature. Sprinkle each piece with confectioners' sugar just before serving.

TIP: *Temperature plays a crucial role in the recipe. First cool the meringue layers enough so they do not melt the butter cream. Then the assembled cake must be chilled enough to cut without shattering. Finally, the cake must be allowed to warm to room temperature for serving.*

CORNMEAL CAKE WITH WARM BERRIES

Artoa Baiarekin

The cornmeal cake of the Aldakurria *cidrerie* just outside of Lasse in the French Basse Navarre province inspired this recipe. It is so flavorful, with a sweet corn taste and a crumbly, dense génoise texture, that the *cidrerie* serves the cake on its own. I like to serve it warm or at room temperature with a fruit compote and a dollop of crème fraîche.

SERVES 8 TO 10

CORNMEAL CAKE

½ pound (2 sticks) unsalted butter, softened, plus more for buttering the baking pan

½ cup flour plus more for dusting the pan

1½ cups yellow cornmeal

2½ teaspoons baking powder

1 cup sugar

4 eggs

Seeds of 1 vanilla bean or ½ teaspoon vanilla extract

2 teaspoons grated lemon zest

BERRY SAUCE

2 tablespoons unsalted butter

2 cups fresh blueberries

1 cup fresh raspberries

2 cups hulled and quartered strawberries

½ cup sugar

1 cup crème fraîche

Preheat the oven to 375 degrees F.

To make the cornmeal cake, butter and flour a 9 × 2½-inch springform pan.

Combine the cornmeal, flour, and baking powder in a small bowl and set aside.

In the work bowl of a standing mixer fitted with the whisk attachment, combine the butter and sugar at high speed until smooth. Beat in the eggs, one at a time, mixing well after each addition. Add the vanilla bean seeds (or extract) and zest. Scrape down the sides of the bowl to ensure that all of the ingredients are evenly incorporated. Working in small batches, add the dry ingredients to the batter and mix on medium speed until well combined. Pour and scrape the batter into the cake pan and give it a shake to level off the batter. Bake in the oven until firm to the touch, or when a knife inserted in the center of the cake comes out clean, 40 to 45 minutes.

Let cool in the pan for 15 to 20 minutes before transferring the cake to a cooling rack.

To make the berry sauce, melt the butter in a large sauté pan over medium heat.

Outside the town of Ainhoa.

Combine the blueberries, raspberries, strawberries, and sugar in a large bowl and toss the ingredients together to coat the fruit with the sugar. Add all of the fruit to the sauté pan and cook just until the fruit begins to soften and break down, 2 to 3 minutes. Stir occasionally. Remove from the heat and set aside to cool for about 10 minutes.

Slice the cake and serve each piece with several heaping spoonfuls of berry sauce and a dollop of crème fraîche.

GÂTEAU BASQUE

Gâteau Basque is a relatively simple, unadorned golden cake that manages to generate an extraordinary amount of comment and argument. Despite the fact that it is made and loved throughout the Basque country, nothing about it is standard, except that two layers of sweet pastry enclose a filling. The pastry may or may not include almonds, and the filling may be pastry cream or Cherry Preserves (page 238), but never both—unless you wish to break with tradition as I do, by adding pitted whole cherries to the pastry cream before baking. One of my wife's and my favorite things to do is to search out different versions of Gâteau Basque. One of the best we have found is from Moulin de Bassilour, a bakery in a charming eighteenth-century flour mill in Bidart, just south of Biarritz. No amount of cajoling would persuade the staff to relinquish their recipe. I was surprised and delighted to find a superb Gâteau Basque made here in San Francisco by Angele Goyenetche, a fellow Basque expatriate. I am so fond of it that it is the only item on Fringale's menu not made in our own kitchen. But she wouldn't divulge her recipe either. I had no choice but to put my pastry training into practice and develop this recipe, which rivals the best of them.

To make the pastry cream, in the work bowl of a standing mixer fitted with the balloon attachment, beat the egg yolks and sugar until frothy. Add the flour and mix these ingredients on medium speed until well combined; set aside.

SERVES 6 TO 8

PASTRY CREAM

2 egg yolks

¼ cup sugar

3 tablespoons flour

1¼ cups milk

½ vanilla bean, split in half lengthwise

DOUGH

8 tablespoons unsalted butter, softened

1 cup sugar

2 egg yolks

1 tablespoon rum

2 teaspoons almond extract

1 teaspoon pastis, such as Ricard or Pernod, or an anise-flavored liqueur

Pinch of kosher salt

Seeds of 1 vanilla bean

1½ cups flour

⅓ cup Ground Almond Powder (page 235)

1 teaspoon baking powder

Butter for buttering the pan

Flour for dusting the pan

1 egg, beaten lightly with a fork, for egg glaze

Bring the milk and vanilla bean to a boil in a large saucepan. As soon as the milk begins to boil, take the pan off the heat, remove the vanilla bean, scrape the seeds out of the pod, and stir them into the milk. Discard the pod.

Pour half the boiling milk into the bowl with the egg and flour mixture while stirring ingredients together briskly with a strong wire whisk. Bring the remaining half of the milk back to a boil. As soon as it boils, pour all of the ingredients from the mixing bowl into the pan of boiling milk while whisking vigorously until smooth. Bring to a boil and stir for 1 minute longer. Remove the pastry cream from the heat and spread it on a sheet pan or in a shallow baking dish to cool. Lay a large sheet of plastic wrap directly on top of the pastry cream and set aside.

To make the dough, in the work bowl of a standing mixer fitted with the paddle attachment, beat the butter and sugar together until well blended. Add the egg yolks one at a time, beating well after each addition. Add the rum, almond extract, pastis, and salt.

Add the vanilla bean seeds, flour, almond powder, and baking powder. Using the paddle attachment, combine the ingredients on low speed until they come together to form a firm dough. Form the dough into 2 even balls, cover with plastic wrap, and refrigerate for 1 hour or more.

Preheat the oven to 350 degrees F.

Butter and flour a 9-inch round cake pan.

Lightly flour a work surface and roll out one of the balls of dough into an 11-inch circle, approximately ⅓ inch thick. Carefully drape the dough over the rolling pin and transfer it to the prepared cake pan; gently press the dough down into the sides of the pan.

Spread the pastry cream in an even layer on top of the pastry dough.

Roll out the remaining ball of dough into a 9-inch circle, ⅓ inch thick. Carefully drape it over the cake pan, on top of the pastry cream, to form the top layer of the cake. Pinch the edges of the dough together to firmly seal in the filling. Trim off any uneven edges. Brush the top of the cake with beaten egg.

Bake until golden brown, 40 to 45 minutes. Set aside to cool for 10 minutes before inverting onto a cooling rack. Turn the cake right side up and let it cool completely. Transfer to a serving plate, and serve at room temperature.

(continued)

VARIATION FOR BASQUE COOKIES

I read about a new bakery just outside of Sare, a town in the Labourd, rumored to make great Gâteaux Basques. When my wife and I found the bakery, Patisserie Haranea, I knocked on the first door I saw and a man came out. Without any warning he blurted, "You are Gerald Hirigoyen." It turned out that he was an old friend from kindergarten whose parents once owned a bakery next to my parents' grocery store in Anglet. While we talked over the past 30 years, he gave us a plate of crunchy almondy cookies. My wife was so impressed that she asked how he made them. He explained that all he did was to roll out the dough trimmings of his Gâteaux Basques and cut them into cookies. You can use the trimmings from this cake or simply make cookies with the dough. In that case, you will have enough dough to make 2 to 3 dozen cookies.

Roll out the dough until ⅓ inch thick and cut into cookie shapes with a knife or cookie cutters. Transfer to a buttered and floured baking sheet and decorate with a few sliced almonds. Brush the cookies with an egg wash and bake in a preheated 350 degrees F. oven until golden brown, about 15 minutes. Cool on a rack, then lightly dust with powdered sugar.

Making the day's supply of Gâteaux Basques at Patisserie Haranea in Sare.

APPLE AND QUINCE TART

This very elegant-looking yet easily made dessert pairs apples, the most widely grown fruit in the Basque region, with the delicately flavored and aromatic quince. The scent of this tart as it bakes is mouthwatering—the essence of autumn.

SERVES 4

2 medium-large apples, peeled, cored, and halved

1 sheet frozen puff pastry, thawed, plus more for making a border

1 egg, lightly beaten for glazing

⅔ cup Quince Puree (page 237)

1 rounded tablespoon sugar

1⅓ tablespoons unsalted butter, cut into small pieces

Preheat the oven to 400 degrees F.

Line a sheet pan with parchment paper; set aside.

Using a mandoline or sharp knife, slice the apples crosswise as thinly as possible; set aside.

Cut the puff pastry dough into an 8 × 8-inch square, then cut 4 strips approximately ¾ × 8 inches. Lay the pastry square on the sheet pan and brush the outer ¾-inch edges of the dough with beaten egg. Lay two of the strips on the opposite outer edges of the base pastry that have been brushed with beaten egg. Dab a little more egg glaze on the four corners of the positioned strips. Lay the 2 remaining strips of pastry across the remaining sides to form a "frame" around the main square of pastry. Pierce the bottom of the dough in many places with a fork, avoiding the sides.

Spread the quince puree over the bottom of the tart, keeping inside the positioned borders. Fan the sliced apple in slightly overlapping rows on top of the quince. Brush all over the top of the tart, including the borders, with the egg glaze. Sprinkle the sugar on top of the apples and scatter the butter evenly over the fruit. Pierce a few holes in the borders with a fork.

Bake until the apples are cooked through and the puff pastry is golden brown, 25 to 30 minutes. The tart is best served warm or at room temperature.

QUINCE AND GOAT CHEESE LAYER CAKE WITH CANDIED PINE NUTS

Irasagar Pastiza Ahuntz-Gasnarekin

After a meal, I sometimes can't decide between a sweet dessert and a cheese plate, which in the Basque country would be served with quince paste or perhaps Cherry Preserves (page 238). This layer cake filled with quince puree and iced with cheese gives me everything at once. It is sweet enough to please with just the right amount of cheese to balance the flavor. Instead of a sheep's milk cheese, I've used a wonderful, fresh goat cheese made in nearby Sonoma County.

SERVES 6 TO 8

GÉNOISE

Butter for buttering the pan

½ cup all-purpose flour, sifted, plus more for dusting the pan

2 large eggs

⅓ cup sugar

GOAT CHEESE ICING

½ pound soft goat cheese

Seeds of ½ vanilla bean

¼ cup sugar

1 cup heavy cream

ASSEMBLY

3 cups Quince Puree (page 237)

PINE NUTS

2 tablespoons Simple Syrup (page 239)

½ cup pine nuts

Preheat the oven to 400 degrees F. Butter and flour a 7-inch springform pan.

Fill a medium saucepan half full of water and bring it to a simmer.

In the work bowl of a standing mixer, combine the eggs and sugar. Place the mixing bowl directly over the pan of simmering water and whisk until the ingredients feel luke-warm. Transfer the mixing bowl to its stand and beat the ingredients on high speed with the whisk attachment until mixture cools and the forms a thick yellow ribbon, about 12 minutes.

Fold the flour into the batter using a rubber spatula. Pour it into the prepared pan and smooth the top. Bake until the cake springs back to the touch, about 15 to 18 minutes. Invert onto a rack, carefully unmold, and let cake cool completely.

To make the goat cheese icing, in the work bowl of a standing mixer fitted with the whisk attachment, beat the goat cheese, vanilla bean seeds, and sugar together on low speed. Add the cream in a slow steady stream until the ingredients are well combined, about 1 minute. Mix on high speed for 15 seconds, then set aside.

To assemble the cake, carefully slice the génoise into four horizontal layers, using a long, serrated knife. Place one layer in the bottom of the same springform mold the génoise was baked in. Spread one-third of the quince puree over the génoise. Repeat twice, and finish with the remaining layer of génoise. Spread the goat cheese in a thick, even layer on top of the last layer of génoise. Scrape away goat cheese above the top of the cake mold.

Cover with plastic wrap and refrigerate until set, 2 to 3 hours.

To toast the pine nuts, combine the simple syrup and the pine nuts in a medium non-stick pan over medium heat. Stir frequently until the sugar "dries out" and the nuts turn golden brown and are caramelized, about 5 minutes. Take care not to overcook the pine nuts, or they will taste bitter. Scrape the candied nuts onto a plate and let cool for 15 to 20 minutes.

To serve the cake, unmold it onto a serving platter and scatter the pine nuts on top of the cake.

CHOCOLATE ROCKS

Txokolate Harkaitza

The shape of these desserts reminds me of the craggy rocks clad in rough coats of seaweed and streaming with surf spume just off the coast of Biarritz. The chocolate meringues are mounded with chocolate mousse and flecked with cocoa just as the rocks are flecked with sea foam.

MAKES 12

MERINGUE

Melted unsalted butter for brushing the pan

3 egg whites

⅔ cup sugar

1 tablespoon cocoa powder

MOUSSE

4 egg yolks

¼ cup plus 2 tablespoons sugar

5 ounces good-quality European semisweet or bittersweet chocolate

1¼ cups (2½ sticks) unsalted butter, cut into cubes

3 egg whites

Confectioners' sugar or cocoa powder for dusting (optional)

Preheat the oven to 275 degrees F.

To make the meringues, line a large sheet pan with parchment paper, and brush it with the melted butter; set aside.

In the work bowl of a standing mixer fitted with a whisk attachment, beat the egg whites to the hard-peak stage while slowly adding ⅓ cup sugar.

Combine the remaining ⅓ cup sugar and the cocoa powder, then fold into the egg whites. Spoon the meringue into 12 individual mounds on the sheet pan.

Bake until the meringues are crisp, approximately 1 hour. Set them aside on a rack for at least 30 minutes.

To make the mousse, in the work bowl of a standing mixer fitted with the whisk attachment, beat the egg yolks and ¼ cup sugar together until frothy and pale yellow.

Melt the chocolate and butter together in the top of a double boiler over gently simmering water, whisking until smooth and creamy. Remove the bowl from the heat, and immediately stir the egg yolk mixture into the chocolate; set aside.

Whip the egg whites to the hard-peak stage, while adding the remaining 2 tablespoons sugar. Gently fold them into the chocolate batter, using a large spatula, just until evenly combined. Place the mousse in the refrigerator until it firms slightly, about 30 minutes.

Carefully shape 2 to 3 rounded tablespoonfuls of the mousse on top of the meringues.

Dust the chocolate "rocks" with confectioners' sugar or cocoa powder, or both. May be served chilled or at room temperature.

BERET BASQUE AU CHOCOLAT

Eskualdun Txapela Xokoletarekin

This typical Basque cake is slightly domed and covered with chocolate curls so that it resembles the daily headgear of Basque men, the black beret or *txapela*. For festivities, the black is exchanged for a red one, worn with a red kerchief at the neck, red sash, and a white shirt and trousers. Two of the best versions of Beret Basque I know are those from Patisserie Dodin in Biarritz and Patisserie Mandion in Anglet. If you make this one, you will have a good standard by which to appreciate theirs when you visit.

SERVES 6 TO 8

GÉNOISE

Butter for buttering the pan

¾ cup all-purpose flour, sifted, plus more for dusting the pan

4 large eggs

½ cup sugar

CHOCOLATE MOUSSE

7 ounces good-quality European semisweet chocolate

4 tablespoons unsalted butter

4 large eggs, separated

½ cup sugar

1 cup heavy cream, whipped into firm peaks

GARNISH

2 cups chocolate curls

Preheat the oven to 400 degrees F. Butter and flour a 9½-inch round glass baking dish; set aside.

Fill a medium saucepan half full of water and bring it to a simmer.

In the work bowl of a standing mixer, combine the eggs and sugar. Place the mixing bowl directly over the pan of simmering water and whisk until the ingredients feel luke-warm. Transfer the mixing bowl to its stand and continue to beat the ingredients on high speed with the whisk attachment until the mixture cools and forms a thick yellow ribbon, about 12 minutes.

Fold the flour into the batter using a rubber spatula. Pour it into the prepared pan and smooth the top. Bake until the cake springs back to the touch, about 15 to 18 minutes. Invert onto a rack, carefully lift off the pan, and let it cool completely.

Cut a cardboard circle 9½ inches in diameter and place the génoise on top it. Starting at the top edge of the cake, carefully cut a concave semicircle out of the cake. If the cake is properly cooled, you should be able to easily lift the semicircle out of the cake. The génoise should now look as if a crater has been carved out of it. Set both the base of the cake and the removed semicircle aside.

Men in traditional dress headed for festivities.

To make the mousse, melt the chocolate and butter together in the top of a double boiler over gently simmering water, whisking until smooth and creamy; set aside.

Whip the egg whites to stiff peaks, while gradually adding ¼ cup of sugar; set aside.

Lightly beat the egg yolks and fold them into the melted chocolate, then stir in the remaining ¼ cup sugar.

Fold the egg whites into the whipped cream a little at a time, then immediately whisk the chocolate mixture into the cream mixture just until incorporated. Do not overmix.

Fill the "crater" of the génoise with the chocolate mousse until it is flush with the top edge of the cake, creating a flat surface. Flip the génoise semicircle over on top of the cake so that it sits like a dome on top of the mousse. Spread the remaining mousse over the top and sides of the cake to bind the two pieces together into one large circular dome, or "beret." Sprinkle chocolate curls over the top and sides of the cake. Refrigerate for 1 to 2 hours before serving. The cake may be served chilled or at room temperature.

BAKED CHOCOLATE CAKE

Txokolate Bizkotxa

Bayonne became the chocolate capital of France in the seventeenth century when Jews, fleeing the Spanish Inquisition, escaped over the Pyrenees passes and settled in *Pays Basque*. For four centuries Bayonnais chocolatiers have specialized in high-quality bitter chocolate. I have kept this cake simple, to celebrate the taste of the chocolate. It has a wonderful moist texture and holds beautifully if you want to make it a day ahead. Serve it warm or cold with a dollop of crème fraîche or whipped cream with perhaps a few ripe berries.

SERVES 6 TO 8

12½ tablespoons unsalted butter, softened, plus more for buttering the pan

⅓ cup flour plus flour for dusting the pan

5¼ ounces good-quality European semisweet or bittersweet chocolate

3 eggs

¾ cup sugar

Preheat the oven to 375 degrees F. Butter and flour an 8-inch square or 9-inch round baking pan.

Combine the butter and chocolate in the top of a double boiler. Place over gently simmering water and whisk until melted and smooth.

In the work bowl of a standing mixer fitted with the whisk attachment, beat the eggs and sugar together until frothy. Add the flour and mix until well combined.

Fold one-third of the chocolate into the egg mixture, using a large rubber spatula, then fold in the remaining chocolate just until incorporated. Take care not to overmix the ingredients.

Pour the batter into the prepared pan, and bake in the oven until a knife, when inserted, comes out clean, 35 to 40 minutes.

Invert onto a rack and let cool to room temperature before serving.

CHOCOLATE TRUFFLES WITH BRANDY

Xokolate Boilak Brandireki

All over the world, Basques follow the old traditions of helping each other. This informal network has aided me several times. The first time was when my uncle introduced me to pastry maker Robert Linxe, who in turn introduced me to master pâtissier Jean Millet in Paris, who hired me immediately. Today, Linxe owns Maison du Chocolat, one of the premier chocolate houses in Paris. Whenever I visit Paris, I stop by to see him and indulge in a few of his scrumptious truffles. He inspired this recipe for the chocolate truffles I serve in our restaurants in San Francisco.

MAKES 60 TO 70 TRUFFLES

1 pound good-quality European semisweet chocolate, finely chopped

1 cup heavy cream

½ cup brandy

1 pound semisweet *couverture* (high-grade chocolate used for coating)

2 cups unsweetened cocoa powder

Place the semisweet chocolate in a large heatproof mixing bowl and set aside.

Combine the cream and brandy in a small saucepan and bring the mixture to a boil. Then pour it into the chocolate and whisk until the ingredients are smooth and the chocolate is totally melted. Leaving the whisk in the bowl, put it directly in the refrigerator for 30 minutes, whisking the ingredients a couple of times every 5 minutes as it cools.

Line a large sheet pan with parchment paper.

Transfer the chocolate mixture to a large pastry bag fitted with a round tip or a strong plastic bag with a corner snipped (it is better to cut the plastic bag after it is filled). Pipe the batter into ¾-inch-diameter balls onto the sheet pan. Refrigerate the truffles until they are cool enough to hold their shape when lifted, 40 to 45 minutes.

Melt the *couverture* in the top of a double boiler over gently simmering water, whisking frequently until smooth and creamy. Remove the pan from the heat and let cool until the chocolate is no longer warm but still liquid enough to coat the truffles.

Place the cocoa powder in a shallow bowl.

First dip the truffles in the *couverture*, then dredge them in the cocoa powder. Store them in a sealed container for up to 1 month in a cool, dry place.

MERINGUE MAKILAS

Makilak Xokolaterekin

These slim little meringue cookies dipped in chocolate are shaped to resemble the emblematic Basque walking stick, or *makila*. For centuries, *makilas* have accompanied Basque shepherds and pilgrims. The *makila* is a beautifully balanced, elegantly decorated wooden walking staff with an engraved metal pommel and point. However, *makila* means "death giver," which lends a clue to the walking stick's secondary function: a weapon. Underneath the handle hides an engraved blade. For two centuries, the Ainciart-Bergara family has followed age-old techniques for making *makilas* in the town of Larressore in the Labourd region. Beautiful, expensive, and status symbols, the walking sticks are made to measure. No two are identical, and the wait for one is usually a year. Winston Churchill, Ronald Reagan, and François Mitterrand have all carried *makilas*.

MAKES 45 TO 50 COOKIES

3 egg whites

2 cups sifted confectioners' sugar

Seeds of ½ vanilla bean

1½ pounds chocolate *couverture*

Preheat the oven to 275 degrees F. Line 2 sheet pans with parchment paper.

In the work bowl of a standing mixer, combine the egg whites, confectioners' sugar, and vanilla bean seeds. Place the bowl directly over a low flame or heat source, and whisk until the mixture reaches body temperature.

Transfer the bowl to the mixing stand. Using the whisk attachment, continue to whip the mixture on high speed until the egg whites are very stiff, about 6 minutes.

Scoop the ingredients into a pastry bag, and pipe as many ½ × 4-inch sticks as will fit onto the sheet pans.

Bake in the oven until the meringues are hard on the outside, but still slightly chewy inside, 35 to 45 minutes. Transfer to a cooling rack.

Place the beignets on a large serving tray and sift confectioners' sugar over them. Beignets can be eaten warm or at room temperature, as well as reheated in a low oven.

TIP: *The oil must be the correct temperature, 375 degrees F. If it is too hot, the beignets will brown too fast and form a crust that will prevent them from expanding. The resulting beignets will be heavy instead of light and feathery. If the oil is too cool, the beignets will absorb the oil and become soggy.*

BASQUE BRIOCHE

This is a brioche-like cake perfumed with anise-flavored pastis, citrus, and rum. The cake probably originated in neighboring Gascony yet is popular across the French Basque provinces. I find it irresistible with morning coffee or as a midafternoon snack.

SERVES 6 TO 8

3½ teaspoons dried yeast

¼ cup warm water

3¾ cups flour

14 tablespoons (1¾ sticks) unsalted butter, softened, plus more for buttering the mold

Zest of 1 lemon

Zest of 1 orange

1 cup sugar

¼ cup rum

¼ cup pastis, such as Ricard or Pernod

5 eggs

Combine the yeast, warm water, and ½ cup of flour in the work bowl of a standing mixer fitted with a dough hook. Mix on medium speed until a dough forms, 1 to 2 minutes. Cover the starter dough with the remaining 3¼ cups flour, and set aside to rise for 30 minutes. The starter should push up through the flour and create a lot of "cracks" on the surface.

Brush the inside of an extra-large (about 2-quart volume) fluted brioche mold with melted butter; set aside.

In a small saucepan over medium heat, combine the lemon and orange zests, sugar, rum, and pastis. Stir constantly until the ingredients reach body temperature and the sugar has dissolved into a syrup; set aside.

Once the starter dough has risen, add 2 eggs, while mixing on low speed. After 45 seconds, add 2 more. Make sure they are well incorporated before adding the last egg.

Add the syrup to the dough a little at a time, while continuing to beat on low over the course of 2 to 3 minutes, in order to maintain the consistency of the dough. The dough should resemble a dense, sticky batter. Then slowly add the butter bit by bit until it is well incorporated.

Pour the dough into the prepared mold and set aside in the warmest part of the kitchen until the dough rises to fill three-quarters of the mold, 1 to 1½ hours.

Preheat the oven to 375 degrees F.

Bake in the oven until a knife inserted into the center comes out clean, about 1¼ hours. If the top starts to darken too rapidly, cover it with a sheet of aluminum foil.

Unmold onto a cooling rack. May be served warm or at room temperature.

Bread baker at Moulin de Bassilour.

PASTRY FRITTERS

When I was a child, it felt like forever before the *merveilles* were served. My mother did not even start to cook them until well after dessert and after-dinner drinks. Today, they would be considered dessert on their own. Though in many ways I have grown up, I still feel the same hungry impatience when these fritters are cooking. They can be served warm or cold. Pile them high on a platter and dust with powdered sugar.

SERVES 6

3 ½ cups all-purpose flour

1 teaspoon baking powder

5 eggs

12 tablespoons (1 ½ sticks) unsalted butter, cut into small pieces

1 cup plus 2 tablespoons sugar

Pinch of kosher salt

1 teaspoon pastis, such as Ricard or Pernod

1 tablespoon rum

Zest of ½ lemon

Zest of ½ orange

4 to 6 cups vegetable or grape seed oil for frying

Confectioners' sugar

Sift the flour and baking powder into the work bowl of a standing mixer fitted with a dough hook. Add the eggs, butter, 2 tablespoons sugar, salt, pastis, rum, and lemon and orange zest. Mix on medium speed until a ball of dough forms, about 1 minute.

Form into a flat ball, cover with plastic wrap, and refrigerate for at least 1 hour.

Heat the oil in a deep fryer or large, heavy-bottomed saucepan to 375 degrees F.

Lightly flour a work surface and roll out the dough to approximately ¼ inch thick.

Line a large sheet pan with parchment paper; set aside.

Using a cookie cutter, or the tip of a knife, cut out various shapes, between 1 and 2 inches in diameter, and place on the sheet pan.

Drop 6 to 7 fritters at a time into the hot oil. Turn them over in the oil after about 1 minute, and fry until lightly browned on both sides, 1 to 1 ½ minutes longer. Remove the fritters with a slotted spoon, and set them aside to drain on paper towels.

Place all of the fritters in a large mixing bowl and gently toss them together with the remaining 1 cup sugar until thoroughly coated. Pile them up high on a serving platter and sift confectioners' sugar over the top.

CRÈME CARAMEL

Koka

Crème caramel is immensely popular on both sides of the French-Spanish border. In fact, it would be unusual to find a Basque menu anywhere without *koka* on it. Chez L'Ami Jean is a small Basque restaurant in Paris that makes one of the best *kokas* I have ever tasted. I used to go there after work when I was a pastry apprentice in Paris. I had very, very little money but I loved the dessert, and luckily it was the least expensive item on the menu. The proprietor, Peyo, eventually became a good friend and mentor. This particular *koka* has a silken texture and floats in a pool of deeply delicious caramel.

SERVES 6 TO 8

1½ cups sugar
2 tablespoons water
3 whole eggs
9 egg yolks
Seeds from 1 vanilla bean
1 cup crème fraîche
3 cups milk

Combine ½ cup sugar and 2 tablespoons water in a small shallow saucepan over medium-high heat. Stir constantly with a wooden spoon until the liquid caramelizes completely, about 2 to 3 minutes. Immediately pour the liquid into a 6½-inch soufflé mold and carefully (don't burn yourself with the hot caramel!) coat the bottom and sides of the mold as evenly as possible; set aside.

Preheat the oven to 375 degrees F.

In a large mixing bowl, using a wire whisk, combine the whole eggs, egg yolks, remaining 1 cup sugar, and vanilla bean seeds until frothy. Add the crème fraîche and milk. Whisk for another minute until well combined. Pour the ingredients into the mold.

Place the mold in a *bain-marie* in a baking pan, adding enough hot water to reach about halfway up the mold, and put it in the oven to bake for 1½ to 2 hours, or until firm throughout.

Allow the crème caramel to cool for 15 to 20 minutes before removing it from the mold onto a serving platter.

CHESTNUT AND CARAMEL CUSTARD

Esneki Flan Gaztainekin

The soft thud of falling chestnuts marks the late fall season in the Basque country. This custard dessert takes advantage of the abundant crop. The cream and chestnuts are pureed together to give the dessert a subtle flavor and a smooth, rich texture.

SERVES 6

13 tablespoons sugar

2 cups heavy cream

15 chestnuts, roasted and shelled

½ vanilla bean, split in half lengthwise

2 whole eggs

3 egg yolks

Preheat the oven to 400 degrees F.

In a small saucepan over high heat, place 5 tablespoons sugar and stir frequently until it caramelizes, 2 to 3 minutes. Divide the caramel among six ¾-cup ramekins (3 × 1¾ inches); set aside to cool.

In a blender or food processor, combine the heavy cream, chestnuts, and vanilla bean seeds on high speed for 1 minute, or just until well combined. Transfer to a medium heavy-bottomed saucepan, and bring to a boil.

In a large mixing bowl, whisk the whole eggs, egg yolks, and 8 remaining tablespoons of sugar until frothy; set aside.

When the chestnut and cream mixture comes to a boil, gradually pour it into the mixing bowl with the eggs, whisking constantly.

Divide the mixture among the six ramekins. Place the ramekins in a shallow baking pan and add enough hot water to reach halfway up the sides of the ramekins. Bake until the custard is firm to the touch, about 35 minutes.

Remove from the oven and transfer the ramekins to a dry surface to cool completely. Cover and refrigerate until well chilled, 2 to 3 hours. To serve, remove the custard from the ramekins by running a hot knife around the edges of the ramekins and inverting each custard onto a plate.

TIP: *You could also use a 1- or 1½-quart soufflé dish instead of individual ramekins. Add another 15 to 20 minutes to the baking time.*

FRIED CREAM SQUARES

If you were to attend the Carnival festivities in Tolosa in Guipúzcoa, you would be able to feast on *leche frita,* this melt-in-your-mouth Spanish dessert. The batter, which must be refrigerated in advance, is often flavored with cinnamon, though I prefer to add vanilla. Make sure to eat the squares hot, as soon as they are ready.

MAKES 2 CUPS

4 cups milk

1 vanilla bean, split in half
lengthwise

1 tablespoon pastis, such as
Ricard or Pernod

8 egg yolks

1 cup granulated sugar

1 cup flour plus more for
dredging

2 quarts (8 cups) vegetable oil
for deep frying

2 eggs, beaten

Confectioners' or granulated
sugar (optional)

In a medium saucepan over high heat, combine the milk, vanilla bean, and pastis; bring to a boil.

In a large mixing bowl, combine egg yolks and sugar and whisk until frothy. Add the 1 cup flour and stir until smooth; set aside.

Once the milk begins to boil, remove it from the heat. Remove the vanilla bean, and using the tip of a small, sharp knife, scrape the seeds directly into the milk. Discard the bean.

Whisk one-third of the hot milk into the egg mixture. Return the saucepan to high heat, and as soon as the mixture boils, pour the contents of the bowl into the saucepan, while whisking constantly. Return to a boil.

As soon as the mixture boils, remove the pan from the heat and pour and scrape the hot milk into a shallow glass baking dish, approximately 9 × 14 inches. The milk should be about 1 inch deep. Refrigerate for at least 2 hours or overnight.

Heat the vegetable oil in a deep fryer or medium-large, deep, heavy-bottomed saucepan to 350 degrees F., or until a crust of bread becomes golden within moments of being dropped into the oil.

Cut the milk into 1-inch cubes.

Working in small batches, dip the cubes on all sides into the beaten egg and roll in the flour; shake off any excess and quickly drop them into the hot oil. Fry just until golden brown, about 1 minute. Using a slotted spoon, transfer the squares onto paper towels and let drain briefly. Garnish with confectioners' or granulated sugar. Serve while hot!

RICE PUDDING WITH DRIED APRICOTS

Arroza Esne eta Arbeletxekoekin

Rice pudding may have fallen out of fashion in the United States, but it remains a standard on Basque restaurant menus as well as for home cooks. This is a flexible recipe that can be adjusted to reflect the season and individual tastes. It can be flavored with vanilla or with almonds. Any kind of dried fruit can be added, including unBasque-like dried cranberries or blueberries or the more Basque-like cherries, prunes, and apricots. Be sure to use a short-grain rice such as Arborio, as it gives the creamiest results.

SERVES 6 TO 8

1½ cups sugar

4 cups milk

⅔ cup Arborio rice

1 vanilla bean, split in half lengthwise

Grated zest of ½ lemon

Grated zest of ½ orange

2 eggs

½ cup dried apricots, finely diced

In a small saucepan over medium-high heat, place ½ cup sugar. Using the back of a spoon, constantly stir the sugar until it caramelizes into a smooth liquid, about 2 to 3 minutes. Pour the caramel into the bottom of a 6½-inch soufflé mold; set aside.

In a medium saucepan over high heat, combine the milk, Arborio rice, vanilla bean, ½ cup sugar, and lemon and orange zest. Bring to a boil, stirring constantly to prevent the mixture from sticking to the bottom.

Reduce the heat and simmer, uncovered, for 25 to 30 minutes. Stir frequently.

Preheat the oven to 375 degrees F.

In a large mixing bowl, whisk together 2 eggs and the remaining ½ cup sugar until very frothy; set aside.

Remove and discard the vanilla bean from the rice mixture. Pour the mixture into the bowl with the eggs. Add the dried apricots, and whisk the ingredients together quickly and vigorously.

Monday market in St.-Jean-Pied-de-Port.

Pour into the mold, and place it in a *bain-marie*. Bake for 40 to 45 minutes, or until a knife, when inserted, comes out clean.

Let cool for 5 minutes. Loosen the pudding from the sides of the mold using a knife blade. Put a large plate face down on top of the mold, then turn them over together, shaking the mold to loosen the pudding. Serve warm or cold.

GOAT'S MILK CUSTARD WITH CARAMELIZED FIGS AND HONEY

Mamia Piku eta Eztiarekin

Mamia is a centuries-old farmstead dessert of sheep's milk and rennet. It was originally made in a *kaiku*, a scoop-shaped wooden milking pitcher, by dropping heated stones, or plunging a hot iron rod, into the milk, giving it a slightly burned taste. *Mamia* is usually served with sugar, fruit, or honey. Unfortunately, very few people produce sheep's milk in the United States, so I have substituted goat's milk with great success. A few Basque shepherds might turn in their graves if they saw this recipe, but they would rest easy once they tasted it. When figs are out of season, serve the custard with other fruits such as bananas, mangoes, or peaches.

SERVES 8

3 gelatin leaves or 3 teaspoons gelatin powder

2 cups goat's milk

2 cups milk

2 tablespoons unsalted butter

16 ripe Black Mission figs, cut in half lengthwise

3½ tablespoons brown sugar

¼ cup honey

Soak the gelatin in a small bowl of cold water for 15 minutes.

Combine the goat's milk and regular milk in a saucepan, and bring to a boil. Add the gelatin and mix well until it has dissolved completely. Pour the mixture into 6- to 8½-cup ramekins or heatproof glasses. Refrigerate until well chilled, at least 2 hours.

Just before serving, melt the butter in a large sauté pan over medium-high heat. As soon as the butter starts to sizzle, add the figs and sprinkle with the sugar. Gently sauté, turning once or twice, until the figs begin to turn golden brown, about 4 minutes. Remove from the heat, and set aside to cool slightly.

Unmold the goat's milk custards into shallow bowls, and top with an even amount of figs and drizzled honey.

WALNUT CREAM

Intxaurkrema

Having grown up in the city, I did not taste this very traditional farmhouse dessert until a few years ago. It is a typically winter dessert, made from walnuts that grow around nearly every farmhouse. It is usually served warm in small bowls, but you can enjoy it warm or cold, on its own, as a topping for ice cream, or as a dipping sauce for cookies and fruit. It is very easy to make and can be prepared several days in advance.

MAKES 2 CUPS

4 cups milk
1 cinnamon stick
1 cup crushed walnuts
½ cup sugar

Combine the milk and cinnamon stick in a medium saucepan over high heat. Bring to a boil, whisking periodically to ensure that the ingredients do not stick to the pan. Add the walnuts and sugar and return to a boil.

Reduce the heat to simmer and cook, uncovered, until the contents reduce by half. Stir frequently to prevent sticking.

Remove from the heat and transfer the ingredients to a bowl. Cool for 20 to 25 minutes. Discard the cinnamon stick. The consistency should resemble thin peanut butter.

CHERRIES IN RED WINE SOUP

Gerezi Beltza Arno Gorriakin

The village of Itxassou in the Labourd province holds an annual cherry festival in June. Thousands of people arrive to celebrate the harvest, during which a feast is served in the courtyard of the village fronton (pelote court). As much as five tons of cherries are sold in the course of the weekend. Most of Itxassou's cherries are eaten fresh or turned into preserves (page 238). This soup provides another way to take advantage of the bounty. The star anise and cloves give spice notes to the red wine sauce. Any ripe, flavorful fruit could be substituted, including peaches in midsummer and pears in the fall. Serve warm or cold with a scoop of Honey Ice Cream (page 218) or crème fraîche.

SERVES 4 TO 6

2½ cups dry red wine

½ cup port

½ cup sugar

1 vanilla bean, split in half lengthwise

2 star anise

Zest of ½ lemon, cut with a lemon zester into long thin spirals, or finely julienned

Zest of ½ orange, cut with a lemon zester into long thin spirals, or finely julienned

2 cloves

2 pounds black cherries, freshly pitted (or unsweetened frozen)

Combine all of the ingredients except the black cherries in a large saucepan, bring to a boil, and simmer for 10 minutes.

Add the cherries and cook for 2 minutes longer. Remove from the heat.

Remove and discard the vanilla bean. A garnish is not necessary; however, a dollop of crème fraîche or a small scoop of honey ice cream would be a nice accompaniment.

WALNUT AND SHEEP'S MILK CHEESE GRATIN

Intxaur Pastiza Idiazabalko Gaztarekin

Walnuts and sheep's milk cheese often appear together in savory Basque recipes. This unusual dessert gratin binds them together in a rich custard. If you leave out all but a tablespoon or two of the sugar, you could serve the gratin as a first course.

SERVES 5 TO 6

Butter for buttering the pan

3 eggs

½ cup sugar

1½ cups heavy cream

1 cup walnuts, finely chopped

4 ounces grated sheep's milk cheese

Preheat the oven to 375 degrees F. Butter a 9½-inch round baking dish.

Whisk together the eggs and sugar until frothy. Add the cream and mix well. Add the walnuts and sheep's milk cheese and stir just to combine. Pour the batter into the prepared baking dish.

Bake until a knife, when inserted, comes out clean, 35 to 40 minutes. Let cool for 10 to 15 minutes before serving. May be served warm or cold.

FRUIT AND CHEESE PLATTER

Ardi Gasnarekin

This is the way a typical Basque meal would end, with a wedge of local sheep's milk cheese and a square of *membrillo* (quince paste), or the local cherry preserves made from the meaty black cherries of Itxassou. It would make a delicious breakfast or lunch, or an easy picnic item as well.

SERVES 4 TO 6

⅔ cup Quince Puree
  (page 237)

⅔ cup Cherry Preserves
  (page 238)

¼ to ½ pound assorted
  sheep's milk cheese, thinly
  sliced

1 fresh baguette or crusty
  bread, cut diagonally in
  ¾-inch-thick slices

Place the quince puree and cherry preserves in small bowls in the center of a large platter and arrange the sliced cheese around the bowls. Serve with the baguette alongside.

HONEY ICE CREAM

Ezti Izozki

Wherever you go in the Basque country, you spot road signs pointing to the nearest honey producer. In markets, honey vendors sell acacia, wildflower, and mountain honey. Yet honey is rarely used in recipes. I love the flavor of honey and the unusual, delicate sweet taste it gives to ice cream.

MAKES 2 TO 3 CUPS

6 egg yolks
¼ cup sugar
2 cups heavy cream
½ cup honey

Beat the eggs and sugar together in a large bowl with a strong wire whisk.

Combine the cream and honey in a large saucepan over high heat, and bring to a boil, whisking periodically to ensure that the ingredients do not stick to the pan.

Once the cream mixture begins to boil, whisk half of it into the bowl with the egg yolks. Return the remaining half in the saucepan to high heat and bring back to a boil. Then pour all of the ingredients from the bowl into the saucepan, mixing constantly with a wooden spoon. Continue to stir over high heat until the mixture is smooth, 1 to 2 minutes longer.

Prepare an ice bath in a large bowl with half ice and half water.

Remove the saucepan from the heat, strain the ingredients into a large bowl, and place the bowl in the ice bath for a few minutes, until the mixture drops to room temperature.

Pour the mixture into an ice cream maker and freeze following the manufacturer's directions. Serve when done or transfer to suitable containers and store in the freezer.

IZARRA ICE CREAM

Izarra ("star" in Basque) is a brandy-based liqueur flavored with as many as 30 or 40 exotic herbs from the Pyrenees. The distillery is in Bayonne and is a popular tourist stop year-round. Izarra, traditionally drunk straight up or over ice, is the most acclaimed *digestif* in the French Basque country. There are two types of Izarra: green, which is stronger and has a pepper and mint taste; and yellow, which is sweeter and based on saffron, bitter almonds, and honey. Both work equally well in this recipe.

MAKES 4 TO 6 CUPS

8 egg yolks

1 cup sugar

4 cups heavy cream

⅓ cup Izarra or Chartreuse liqueur

In a large bowl, combine the egg yolks and sugar; whisk together well.

In a large saucepan over high heat, combine the cream and Izarra and bring to a boil, whisking periodically to ensure that it does not stick.

Once the mixture boils, whisk half of the hot cream into the egg yolk mixture.

Return the remaining cream in the saucepan to high heat and bring it back to a boil. Pour the cream and egg mixture into the saucepan, mixing constantly with a wooden spoon. Continue stirring over high heat until the mixture is smooth, 1 to 2 minutes.

Prepare an ice bath with half ice and half water in a large bowl; set aside.

Strain the custard into a large bowl and place the bowl directly in the ice bath until the temperature of the liquid drops to room temperature, 2 to 3 minutes.

Pour the mixture into an ice cream maker and freeze according to the manufacturer's directions. Serve when done or transfer to suitable containers and store in the freezer.

GREEN APPLE SORBET

Liquor de Manzana, a favorite liqueur of the Basque provinces made from green apples, is served very cold in short glasses. It makes a refreshing sorbet.

SERVES 4 TO 6

1½ pounds green apples, peeled, cored, and quartered

1½ cups Simple Syrup (page 239)

1½ cups water

⅓ cup Liquor de Manzana, or other apple-flavored spirit, or vodka

Put the apples, simple syrup, and water in a medium saucepan and bring to a slow boil over medium-high heat, stirring frequently. Simmer until the apples are soft and cooked through, about 10 minutes.

Transfer the ingredients to a blender or food processor and puree on high speed to a creamy consistency. Add the Liquor de Manzana and blend for 15 seconds.

Place in the container of an ice cream machine and freeze according to the manufacturer's instructions. Serve when done or transfer to suitable containers and store in the freezer.

Opposite page, left to right: Green Apple Sorbet, Patxaran Sorbet, Poire William Sorbet

POIRE WILLIAM SORBET

Udare Jela

SERVES 6 TO 8

½ cup sugar

2 cups water

1¼ pounds comice pears, peeled, cored, and quartered

½ cup Poire William eau-de-vie

Martine Brana produces some of the finest eaux-de-vie (clear, distilled fruit brandies) I have tasted. She learned the art of distillation from her father, who ran the family wine *négociant* business in St.-Jean-Pied-de-Port. After extensive travels to study eaux-de-vie, he returned to begin making his own. He planted a pear orchard and made his own eaux-de-vie from pears, plums, and raspberries. Martine's brother, Jean, makes the red and white Irouleguy wines from the family's steeply terraced vineyards. If you cannot find the Poire William from Brana, you can substitute any of the other fine pear eaux-de-vie made in Europe—and now in California, too—or vodka would work as well.

Combine the sugar, water, and pears in a saucepan, and bring to a boil. Simmer until the pears are soft and cooked through, about 10 minutes. Transfer the ingredients to a blender and puree on high speed for 30 seconds. You should have about 4 cups of liquid.

Stir in the Poire William.

Place in the container of an ice cream machine and freeze according to the manufacturer's instructions. Serve when done or transfer to a suitable container and store in the freezer.

PATXARAN SORBET

Made in the Spanish Basque province of Navarra, Patxaran liqueur has a delicious light taste of sloe berries and anise. It is usually served chilled and over ice and makes a terrific, pale pink sorbet. If you cannot find it at your local wine and spirits shop, you can substitute a good-quality anise-flavored liqueur.

SERVES 4 TO 6

½ cup Patxaran liqueur

1 ½ cups Simple Syrup (page 239)

1 cup water

Combine all of the ingredients in a bowl and whisk together well.

Pour the mixture into the container of an ice cream machine and freeze according to the manufacturer's instructions. Serve when done or transfer to a suitable container and store in the freezer.

Homemade quince paste and cider for sale.

TURRON PARFAIT

Turron

When my sister, Anita, and I used to cross into Spain to shop, our favorite purchase was *turron*, Spanish nougat. When we returned home, I hid mine because Anita would immediately finish hers and come looking for mine. Made from almonds, honey, and egg whites, it can be formed in either a hard or soft style. In French Basque country, there is yet another version of *turron* that is similar to marzipan. It is made in long loaves studded with fruits and nuts, then sliced to show off the colorful patterns. This recipe makes a creamy frozen dessert that looks very pretty in tall, decorative parfait glasses. It's terrific for a party, since it can be made well ahead of time.

SERVES 6 TO 8

1 cup or 7 ounces *turron* (or marzipan)

⅓ cup amaretto liqueur

4 egg yolks

½ cup Simple Syrup (page 239), hot

2 cups heavy cream

½ cup candied almonds (see Tip)

Beat the *turron* and amaretto together in a large mixing bowl until creamy, removing some, but not all, of the lumps. Set aside.

Fill a medium saucepan half full of water and bring to a gentle simmer over medium-high heat.

Place the egg yolks in a heatproof mixing bowl. Put the bowl over the simmering water. While whisking vigorously, slowly pour the hot syrup into the egg yolks. Continue to whisk vigorously until the ingredients are frothy and stiff, about 3 to 4 minutes. Remove the bowl from over the water and beat with an electric mixer on high speed until the ingredients cool considerably, about 5 minutes.

Place the heavy cream in a separate bowl, and using an electric mixer or wire whisk, beat until soft peaks form.

Fold the cooled egg mixture into the bowl with the *turron* and amaretto until well combined. Fold in the heavy cream until evenly blended.

Bayonne Cathedral.

Divide the mixture between six to eight parfait glasses. Cover the glasses and freeze for 4 hours or, preferably, overnight.

Remove from the freezer a few minutes before serving and garnish with candied almonds.

TIP: *You can candy any nut with this method. Combine ½ cup almonds with 2 tablespoons simple syrup (page 239) in a medium nonstick pan. Place over medium heat and stir frequently until sugar "dries out" and the nuts begin to brown and caramelize, about 5 minutes. Scrape the nuts onto a plate to cool.*

RENDERED DUCK FAT

Some things are above politics, both governmental and gastronomical, and duck fat should be one of them. Foods, especially potatoes, cooked in duck fat are simply too delicious to be discriminated against for any reason! In the cooking of southwest France, of which *Pays Basque* is a part, goose and duck fat are the cooking fats of choice. In *Pays Basque*, as in early America, we also cook with freshly rendered pork fat. It, too, adds its own wonderful rich flavor to foods. You can buy rendered duck fat from specialty grocers or butchers, but it is easy to do at home.

MAKES ABOUT 2 CUPS

All of the skin and fat from 2 large ducks (about 2 pounds of skin fat)

Preheat the oven to 375 degrees F.

Cut the skin and fatty tissue into small pieces.

Place the skin and fatty tissue in an ovenproof casserole and bake for 1½ hours.

Pour the fat through a fine-mesh sieve into a large container. Set aside to cool completely.

Store in the refrigerator for up to 3 months or in the freezer for up to 1 year.

TIP: *Use the duck to make a classic pot-au-feu. Make a court bouillon with vegetables, then cook the duck in it. You could also confit the duck in the rendered fat, but I prefer to confit duck with the skin on (page 124). Then you have a crispy brown skin on the duck to sink your teeth into.*

BASQUAISE SAUCE

Endless and delicious variations of this sauce exist in Basque country. I developed this recipe as a way to impart the flavor of Basque cuisine to many foods. It is related to the Basque classic *Pipérade* (page 46) but is more convenient and even more versatile. It can be used as a sauce for pasta or vegetables and even as a barbecue sauce. Thinned with a little water, it can be used to poach fish or chicken breasts. With a little vinegar added, it becomes a salad dressing. And it can be made ahead and frozen, so a simple and tasty meal can be put together with very little effort.

MAKES 2 TO 3 CUPS

- 3 tablespoons olive oil
- 1 medium onion, coarsely chopped
- 3 small red bell peppers, cored, and coarsely chopped (page 233)
- 5 garlic cloves
- 4 tomatoes, coarsely chopped
- 1 bouquet garni
- ⅛ teaspoon *piment d'Espelette*
- 1 teaspoon kosher salt
- ¼ teaspoon freshly ground white pepper
- ⅓ cup water

Warm the olive oil in a large saucepan over high heat. Add the onion, bell peppers, and garlic and sauté over medium-high heat until golden, about 10 minutes.

Add the tomatoes, bouquet garni, *piment d'Espelette*, salt, pepper, and ⅓ cup water; bring to a boil. Reduce the heat to medium, cover, and simmer gently until the mixture thickens, about 45 minutes.

Working in small batches, transfer the ingredients to a blender or food processor fitted with a metal blade and puree until the sauce is smooth, about 2 minutes. Season with salt and pepper to taste. Use immediately or store in an airtight container in the refrigerator for up to 1 week. Can be frozen for up to 3 months.

Drying peppers.

ROASTED PEPPERS

Fresh peppers

It is worth taking a trip to the town of Lodosa in Navarra in October simply to smell the mouthwatering aroma of the *piquillo* peppers roasting over open wood fires. I do prefer the smoky taste of peppers charred over an open flame. When selecting peppers to roast, look for ones without deep lobes on the bottom. (Those with deep lobes are more difficult to peel.) Experiment with roasting all the varieties of peppers and chiles you find at your farmers' market. If the peppers are thin-fleshed, use extra care in the charring, or you will have burned, not roasted, peppers.

Place the peppers directly over a medium flame or under a preheated broiler, turning them with tongs every few minutes, until the skins are evenly blistered and have turned a black-brown color.

Remove the peppers from the flame, and place them in a paper bag. Close the bag, allowing the peppers to steam for 5 to 10 minutes. Remove them from the bag, quickly peel away the burned outer skins, and remove the seeds.

CORN GALETTES

This old-fashioned, traditional bread plays the same role in Basque cuisine that the tortilla plays in Mexican cuisine. Like the tortilla, the breads are cooked on an iron griddle, where they tend to puff up and then collapse as they cool. The dark, almost burned spots on the *taloa* indicate that they have been correctly made. Beer provides the only leavening. In the old days, mill workers and farmers often made a meal of *taloa* soaked in a bowl of milk—a sort of Basque milk toast. Now *taloa* are served with charcuterie or stuffed with cheese. They even become dessert when spread with Cherry Preserves (page 238) and served alongside a foamy, steaming cup of hot chocolate. I like to serve them warm with soups, the Bayonne Ham and Sheep's Milk Cheese Terrine (page 58), Tuna Confit (page 68), and just about anything normally served with bread.

MAKES 16 TO 20

1⅔ cups whole wheat or all-purpose flour

1¾ cups corn flour plus more for dusting

4 tablespoons (½ stick) unsalted butter, at room temperature, cut into small pieces

2 tablespoons olive oil

1 teaspoon salt

1 cup warm water

¼ cup beer

In the work bowl of a standing mixer fitted with the paddle attachment, combine the wheat flour and 1¾ cups corn flour. Add the butter, oil, and salt. Mix on low speed until the ingredients are evenly incorporated, 2 to 3 minutes. Slowly add the water and the beer. Continue mixing until the dough is formed and pulls away from the sides of the bowl.

Pat the dough into a ball, place it in a shallow dish, and cover with a kitchen towel. Let the dough rest for 1 hour.

Preheat the oven to 475 degrees F. Line a sheet pan with parchment paper and scatter a dash of corn flour on top; set aside. Lightly flour a work surface with the corn flour.

Roll out the dough ⅛ inch thick. Using a cookie cutter or sharp knife, cut out 4-inch circles and arrange them on the prepared sheet pan.

Bake the galettes for 5 minutes. Turn them over and bake for another 5 minutes. They should be nicely browned with dark spots here and there.

TIP: *You could also cook these galettes on the stove top. Simply warm 1 teaspoon of olive oil in a nonstick sauté pan over high heat and sauté three or four at a time for about 2½ minutes on each side.*

GROUND ALMOND POWDER

Arbendel Irina

This powder can sometimes be found in specialty groceries, but it is very easy to make at home from blanched almonds. Just enough sugar is added to prevent the nuts from getting oily. I like to keep a tub of almond powder in the kitchen to add to pastries, to make an almond crust for fish, or to stuff a lamb shoulder (page 142).

MAKES: SLIVERED ALMONDS, 2⅓ CUPS. SLICED, BLANCHED ALMONDS, 1½ CUPS. WHOLE ALMONDS, 2½ CUPS

2 cups sliced, slivered, or whole blanched almonds

2 tablespoons sugar

Place the nuts and sugar in the bowl of a food processor fitted with the metal blade.

Grind or process the nuts just until they turn into a fine granular powder, about 30 to 45 seconds.

TIP: *Be careful not to overprocess the almonds, or they might turn into a paste instead of a light, granular powder.*

ROASTED CHESTNUTS

Chestnuts

Peeling and eating roasted chestnuts should be declared a Basque national pastime. Families and friends gather to eat the warm nuts, drink wine, and share gossip. Soon a party atmosphere takes over. Fresh chestnuts can be found in markets during the fall and winter. Since roasting them yourself can be time-consuming, I often recommend using the vacuum-packed, prepared nuts available in specialty grocery stores. They are of very high quality and many chefs, including me, use them with great success.

Preheat the oven to 400 degrees F.

With a sharp knife, cut an *X* on the round side of each chestnut. Scatter the chestnuts in a shallow baking dish. Roast in the oven just until the shells start to crack open, 15 to 20 minutes, shaking the pan once or twice.

As soon as they are cool enough to handle, quickly remove the shell and peel away the inner skin. Store, tightly covered, in the freezer (they keep from 6 months up to 1 year.)

Whole chestnuts on the ground.

QUINCE PUREE

Few things please me as much as sitting down to a loaf of fresh bread, a few slices of Basque cheese, and a mound of this quince puree. In Spanish Basque country, *pais vasco*, a sweet quince paste, *membrillo*, is served with sheep's milk cheese. On the French side, *Pays Basque*, the same paste is called *pâte de coing*. Quince, introduced to the Basque provinces in the fifteenth century, ripens in the autumn. Quinces are often displayed in bowls so their scent can perfume the house. When ripe, quinces should be yellow and still very hard to the touch. They are usually furry and sticky and need to be well scrubbed before cooking. Quinces have the seemingly magical ability to turn pink as they cook. This is especially apparent in jelly making, but this puree, too, has a sort of pink-tan color. The delicate, floral, almost citrusy flavor of quince suits this puree to sweet as well as savory dishes such as Salmis of Squab Marinated in Red Wine (page 127), and Fillet of Venison with Quince (page 132).

MAKES 4 CUPS

6 medium quince (about 2½ pounds), well scrubbed, cored, and quartered

1½ cups sugar

1 cup water

1 vanilla bean, split in half lengthwise

Combine the quinces, sugar, and 1 cup water in a large saucepan over medium-high heat.

Scrape the seeds from the vanilla bean and drop into the pan along with the entire pod. Bring to a slow boil, cover, and let simmer, stirring occasionally, until the quinces are cooked through and very tender, about 25 minutes. Remove and discard the vanilla bean.

Working in batches, transfer the quinces to a blender or food processor; blend on high speed until creamy and evenly pureed. Transfer the puree to a large glass bowl and set it aside until it reaches room temperature. Store in the refrigerator for 3 to 4 days, or freeze for up to 6 months.

CHERRY PRESERVES

Cherries grow abundantly in the Basque country, especially in the French province of Labourd, which hugs the Bay of Biscay. The cherries are dark red, meaty, and very flavorful. These preserves are made throughout the countryside and are frequently served with sheep's milk cheese as a dessert (page 217), as a filling for Gâteau Basque (page 186), or on toast for breakfast. No pectin is added, so expect the preserves to be a little runny. Look for large, meaty, and very sweet cherries in order to make this recipe. I find that ripe, sweet Bings work very well.

MAKES 2 TO 3 CUPS

4½ cups sugar

1 cup water

2 pounds pitted
cherries (about 6 cups)

Combine the sugar and water in a large saucepan over high heat and cook until the sugar reaches the "hard ball" stage on a candy thermometer (255 degrees F.).

Add the cherries and return to a boil.

Reduce the heat to medium and stir constantly for 20 minutes. To test for doneness, drizzle ½ teaspoon of the preserve onto a tilted plate. It should run down the plate a little more slowly than if it were water.

Remove from the heat and set aside to cool for 10 to 15 minutes.

Spoon into jars with airtight lids. Cool to room temperature, and store in the refrigerator for 3 to 6 months.

*Local sheepherder
and cheese maker.*

SIMPLE SYRUP

Ur-azukria

Pastry chefs (and I am one by training) consider simple syrup their basic "stock." It is used to moisten cakes; to make parfaits, ice cream, sorbets, and meringues; and even to roast nuts. It is also an elegant way to sweeten iced tea and mixed drinks and cocktails. Refrigerated, it will keep almost indefinitely.

MAKES ABOUT 4 CUPS

4 cups sugar
2 cups water

Combine the sugar and water in a small saucepan over high heat. Bring to a boil, stirring constantly to dissolve the sugar. Once the syrup boils, remove from the heat and cool to room temperature.

Store in a covered glass bottle or container in the refrigerator.

CULINARY GUIDE TO THE BASQUE COUNTRY

RESTAURANTS

LABOURD

PANTXUA
Socoa-Ciboure, France
Tel: (05) 59 47 13 73

LE KAIKU
17, rue de la République,
St.-Jean-de-Luz, France
Tel: (05) 59 26 13 29

LA TABLE DES FRÈRES IBARBOURE
Maricharenia, chemin d'Izengabea,
Guethary-Bidart, France
Tel: (05) 59 54 81 64/59 47 71 62

AUBERGE DE LA GALUPE
Place du Port, Urt, France
Tel: (05) 59 56 21 84
Chef Christian Parra

BISTROT BELLEVUE
5, place Bellevue, Biarritz, France
Tel: (05) 59 24 19 53
Chef Didier Oudil

LA ROTONDE
Hotel du Palais
1, avenue Impératrice
Biarritz, France
Tel: (05) 59 41 64 00
Chef Jean-Marie Gautier

CAMPAGNE ET GOURMANDISES
52, avenue Alan Seeger
Biarritz, France
Tel: (05) 59 41 10 11
Chef André Gaüzere

LES PLATANES
32, avenue Beau-Soleil
Biarritz, France
Tel: (05) 59 23 13 68
Chef Arnaud Daguin

LA GOULUE
3, rue Etienne Ardoin
Biarritz, France
Tel: (05) 59 24 90 90

LE CHEVAL BLANC
rue Bourgneuf, Bayonne, France
Tel: (05) 59 59 01 33
Chef Jean-Claude Telletchea

FRANÇOIS MIURA
24, rue Marugo, Bayonne, France
Tel: (05) 59 59 49 89

RESTAURANT EUZKADI
rue Principale, Espelette, France
Tel: (05) 59 93 91 88
Proprietor André Darraïdou

RESTAURANT ITHURRIA
rue Principale, Ainhoa, France
Tel: (05) 59 29 92 11

LE MOULIN D'ALOTZ
Arcangues, France
Tel: (05) 59 43 04 54

XIXTABERRI—A FARM-AUBERGE
IN THE COUNTRY
Cambo-les-Bains, France
Tel: (05) 59 29 85 36 or 59 29 22 66
Proprietor Maialen Noblia

LE ROUGE ET LE BLANC
87 Avenue de la Marne
64200 Biarritz
Tel: (05) 59 22 16 04
Chef: Pascal Hirigoyen

BASSE NAVARRE

RESTAURANT LES PYRÉNÉES
19, place du Général-de-Gaulle
St.-Jean-Pied-de-Port, France
Tel: (05) 59 37 01 01
Chef Firmin Arrambide

RESTAURANT ARCÉ
St.-Etienne-de-Baïgorry, France
Tel: (05) 59 37 40 14
*Closed mid-November to
mid-March.*
Chef Pascal Arcé

SOULE

RESTAURANT CHILO
Barcus, France
Tel: (05) 59 28 90 79
Chef Pierre Chilo

GUIPÚZCOA

ELKANO
2, calle Herrerieta, Guetaria, Spain
Tel: (34 943) 14 16 14

CASA NICOLASA
4 Aldamar (next to the La Brecha
market), San Sebastián, Spain
Tel: (34 943) 42 17 62

RAMÓN ROTETA
1 Irun, Hondarribia, Spain
Tel: (34 943) 64 16 93

REKONDO
57 Paseo de Igueldo
San Sebastián, Spain
Tel: (34 943) 21 29 07

RESTAURANTE MARTIN
BERASATEGUI
4 Loidi Kalea, Lasarte, Spain
Tel: (34 943) 36 64 71
Chef Martin Berasategui

ARZAK
21 Alto de Miracruz
San Sebastián, Spain
Tel: (34 943) 27 84 65
Chefs Juan Mari and Elena Arzak

AKELARE
56 Paseo Padre Orcolaga
San Sebastián, Spain
Tel: (34 943) 21 20 52
Chef Pedro Subijana

ZUBEROA
8 Barrio Iturrioz, Oyarzun, Spain
Tel: (34 943) 49 12 28
Chef Hilario Arbelaitz

UREPEL
3 Paseo de Salamanca
San Sebastián, Spain
Tel: (34 943) 42 40 40

KARLOS ARGUINANO
13 Mendilauta, Zarautz, Spain
Tel: (34 943) 83 01 78

VIZCAYA

CAFÉ IRUÑA
5 calle Berastegui, Bilbao, Spain
Tel: (34 94) 424 9140

ZORTZIKO
17 Alameda de Mazarredo
Bilbao, Spain
Tel: (34 94) 423 9743

RESTAURANTE ARRIEN
1 El Ferial, Gernika, Spain
Tel: (34 94) 625 0641

GOIZEKO KABI
4 Particular de Estraunza
Bilbao, Spain
Tel: (34 94) 441 5004

RETOLAZA
1 calle de la Tenderia, Bilbao, Spain
Tel: (34 94) 415 0643

NAVARRA

OTANO
5 calle San Nicolas
Pamplona, Spain
Tel: (34 943) 22 50 95 / 22 70 36

PARIS, FRANCE

AU BASCOU
38, rue Réaumur
Tel: 42 72 69 25

CHEZ L'AMI JEAN
27, rue Malat
Tel: 47 05 86 89

BOULANGERIE POUJAURAN
20, rue Jean Nicot
Tel: 47 05 80 88

BAKERIES

MAISON ADAM
6, place Louis XIV
St.-Jean-de-Luz, France
Tel: (05) 59 26 03 54

MOULIN DE BASSILOUR
Arbonne, France
Tel: (05) 59 41 94 49

PATISSERIE HARANEA ET ECO-MUSÉE
Quartier Haranea
Sare, France
Tel: (05) 59 54 22 09
Pastry Chef Vincent Marichular

CHOCOLATE AND TURRON

CAZENAVE
19, rue Port-Neuf, Bayonne, France
Tel: (05) 59 59 03 16

DARANATZ
15, Arceaux Port-Neuf
Bayonne, France
Tel: (05) 59 59 03 55
Well known for its turron.

CHOCOLATS HENRIET
16, avenue Beau Rivage
Biarritz, France
Tel: (05) 59 23 04 10

PATISSERIE MANDION
R.N. (Route National) 10,
Carrefour Anglet, France
Tel: (05) 59 63 86 16

MUSEUM OF CHOCOLATE
4, avenue de la Marne
Biarritz, France
Tel: (05) 59 24 50 50

CHEESE MAKING
RONCAL

ONKIZU
3143 Vudangoz, Navarra, Spain
Tel: (34 948) 47 70 13

OSSAU IRATY, KAIKOU, P'TIT BASQUE

FROMAGERIE PYRENEFROM
Larceveau, Basse Navarre, France
Tel: (05) 59 37 81 13

IDIAZABAL

QUESERIA GAZTADEGUI DERREA
Valle Basaburua
Udabe, Navarra, Spain
Tel: (34 948) 50 31 60

PUR BREBIS

ARDIGASNA S.A.R.L.
Abbaye de Belloc, Urt
Labourd, France
Tel: (05) 59 29 65 55

ETORKI

ETORKI
29, boulevard Gambetta
Mauléon, Soule, France
Tel: (05) 59 28 07 98

LA ROUTE DU FROMAGE
(ST.-JEAN-DE-LUZ TO L'AUBISQUE)
For information call the Syndicat de
Défense de l'AOC
Ossau-Iraty-Brebis-Pyrénées
Tel: (05) 59 80 70 36

HONEY

MIEL LOREZTIA
Jacques Salles
8, avenue des Prés, Bayonne, France
Tel: (05) 59 55 49 14

WINES AND SPIRITS

DOMAINE ETIENNE BRANA
3 bis avenue Jai Alai
St.-Jean-Pied-de-Port, France
Producers of Eaux-de-vie de
Poire William, Irouleguy.
Free tours every day in July and August.
Tel: (05) 59 37 00 44

IZARRA
9, quai Bergeret, Bayonne, France
Tel: (05) 59 55 09 45

MAYOR DE MIGUELOA
Laguardia, Spain
Tel: (34 941) 12 11 75

TXAKOLI TXOMIN ETXANIZ
Caerio Gurutze, Aldamar 33
Guetaria, Spain
Tel/Fax: (34 943) 83 27 02
(or 14 07 02)

MARQUES DE RISCAL
Torrea–1 Elciego, Spain
Tel: (34 941) 10 60 00

REMELLURI
Labastida, Spain
Tel: (34 941) 33 12 74

CAVE D'IROULEGUY
St.-Etienne-de-Baïgorry, France
Tel: (05) 59 37 41 33
*Wine tastings year round. Guided visits
through the vines and wine cellars June to
September.*

CIDRERIES

CIDRERIE ALDAKURRIA
Munoa Iribarne, Lasse, France
Tel: (05) 59 37 13 13

SAGARZAZU
Hondarribia, Spain
Tel: (34 943) 64 16 41

OTHER

MAISON AROSTÉGUY
5, avenue Victor Hugo
Biarritz, France
Tel: (05) 59 24 00 52
*One-stop shopping for regional
gastronomic delights, often called the
Basque "Fauchon."*

MAKILAS

AINCIART-BERGARA
Larressore, France
Tel: (05) 59 93 03 05

BAYONNE HAM

PIERRE OTEIZA
Route de Urepel
Les Aldudes, France
Tel: (05) 59 37 56 11
*Highly regarded Bayonne and Ibaiona
hams made in the Spanish style.*

CHEZ MONTAUSER
17, rue de la Salie
Bayonne, France
Tel: (05) 59 59 07 68

CHEZ SAUVEUR MAYTÉ
St.-Jean-le-Vieux, France
Tel: (05) 59 37 10 02

TRADITIONAL OPEN MARKETS

ANGLET: *Every Thursday morning*

BAYONNE: *Every morning*

BIARRITZ: *Every morning*

CIBOURE: *Every Sunday morning*

ESPELETTE: *Every Wednesday morning*

ST.-JEAN-DE-LUZ: *Every Tuesday and Friday morning*

ST.-JEAN-PIED-DE-PORT: *Every Monday*

SAN SEBASTIÁN: *La Brecha market open Monday through Saturday mornings*

ORDIZIA: *Every Wednesday morning*

BILBAO: *La Ribera Market open Monday through Saturday mornings*

GUERNICA: *Every Monday*

BASQUE LINENS

JEAN VIER LINENS/TABLEWARE
Ecological Museum
Ferme Berrain, Route National 10
St.-Jean-de-Luz, France
Tel: (05) 59 51 06 06

MAISON DE BLANC BERROGAIN
Place des 5 Cantons
Bayonne, France
Tel: (05) 59 59 16 18

CHERBACHO-INCHAUSPÉ
16, rue d'Espagne
St.-Jean-Pied-de-Port, France
Tel: (05) 59 37 18 84

TOURIST BOARDS

COMMERCIAL OFFICE OF SPAIN
405 Lexington Avenue, 44th floor,
New York, NY 10174
Tel: (212) 661-2787
Fax: (212) 867-6055

FRENCH-BASQUE TOURIST BUREAU
(LABOURD, BASSE NAVARRE, SOULE)
Tel: (05) 59 46 46 64

NAVARRA TOURIST BUREAU
(NAVARRA)
Tel: (34 948) 10 77 53

EUSKADI TOURIST BUREA
(GUIPÚZCOA, VIZCAYA, ALAVA)
Tel: (34 943) 42 62 82

PUBLICATIONS

PAYS BASQUE MAGAZINE
(issued in French)
For subscriptions, contact:
Tel: (05) 61 76 64 11
Fax: (05) 61 76 65 67

SPAIN GOURMETOUR
(issued in English)
405 Lexington Avenue, 44th floor,
New York, NY 10174
Tel: (212) 661-4959
Fax: (212) 972-2494

WEBSITE

www.icex.es/repertorios/english/menuprin.html

INTERESTING WORDS OR EXPRESSIONS IN BASQUE

RESTAURANT: *Jatetxea*

BREAKFAST: *Gosaria*

LUNCH: *Bazkaria*

DINNER: *Afaria*

FISH: *Arraina*

BREAD: *Ogia*

BAKERY: *Okindegia*

MARKET: *Merkatua*

PIMENT D'ESPELETTE: *Ezpeletako biperra*

BAYONNE HAM: *Baionako urdaiazpikoa*

OCEAN: *Itsasoa*

"HELLO, HOW ARE YOU?": *"Egun on, nola zaude?"*

"I WOULD LIKE A GLASS OF WATER": *"Baso bat ur nahi nuke, plazer baduzu."*

"WHAT NICE WEATHER WE'RE HAVING TODAY!": *"Gaur, denbora ederra!"*

"COULD I HAVE A GLASS OF CHILLED ROSÉ?": *"Ardo gorri freskua, plazer baduzu?"*

AND RELATED ITEMS

*Note: For certain items we've
indicated wholesale distributors
as well as retailers.*

CHEESE

BELLWEATHER FARMS
9999 Valley Ford Road
Petaluma, CA 94952
Tel: (707) 763-0993
Retailer/Distributor

DEAN & DELUCA
560 Broadway
New York, NY 10012
Tel: (800) 999-0306
Fax: (212) 226-2003
Catalog: (800) 221-7714
*Retail Stores in New York; California;
Washington, D.C.; North Carolina;
Missouri.*

IDEAL CHEESE SHOP, LTD.
1205 Second Avenue
New York, NY 10021
Tel: (800) 382-0109/ (212) 688-7579

LA ESPAÑOLA MEATS, INC.
25020 Doble Avenue
Harbor City, CA 90710
Tel: (310) 539-0455
Fax: (310) 539-5989
Retailer/Distributor

BALDUCCI'S
11–02 Bridge Plaza South, Long
Island City, NY 11101
Tel: (800) 225-3822
Retailer

WHOLE FOODS MARKETS
(NATIONWIDE)
Website: www.wholefoods.com
Retailer

PIMENT D'ESPELETTE

IGO FOODS
P.O. Box 77878
San Francisco, CA 94107
Tel: (888) IGO-9966
Retailer

PIQUILLO PEPPERS

(Note: Look for *"Denomination
Origin del Pimiento del Piquillo de
Lodosa"* on the label to ensure a
top-quality product.)

THE SPANISH TABLE
1427 Western Avenue
Seattle, WA 98101
Tel: (206) 682-2827
E-mail: tablespan@aol.com

ZINGERMAN'S
422 Detroit Street
Ann Arbor, MI 48104
Tel: (888) 636-8162
Tel: (800) 541-2233
Retailer

MIGUEL & VALENTINO
P.O. Box 2102, Baltimore, MD 21203
Tel: (410) 837-7850
Fax: (410) 685-1961
Retailer/Distributor

OKOKI, INC.
175 Graham Street
Stratford, CT 06497
Tel: (203) 378-3700
Fax: (203) 377-9590
Distributor

ELVERS

Okoki, Inc.
175 Graham Street
Stratford, CT 06497
Tel: (203) 378-3700
Fax: (203) 377-9590
Distributor

DOMESTIC BAYONNE-STYLE HAM

D'ARTAGNAN
280 Wilson Avenue
Newark, NJ 07105
Tel: (800) 327-8246
Website: www.dartagnan.com
Retailer/Distributor

DUCK FAT

D'ARTAGNAN
280 Wilson Avenue
Newark, NJ 07105
Tel: (800) 327-8246
Website: www.dartagnan.com
Retailer/Distributor

WHOLE FOODS MARKETS
(NATIONWIDE)
Website: www.wholefoods.com
Retailer

DEAN & DELUCA
560 Broadway, New York, NY 10012
Tel: (800) 999-0306
Fax: (212) 226-2003
Catalog: (800) 221-7714
Retail Stores in New York; California; Washington, D.C.; North Carolina; Missouri.

CHORIZO AND BASQUE SAUSAGE

OKOKI, INC.
175 Graham Street
Stratford, CT 06497
Tel: (203) 378-3700
Fax: (203) 377-9590
Distributor

LA ESPAÑOLA MEATS, INC.
25020 Doble Avenue
Harbor City, CA 90710
Tel: (310) 539-0455
Fax: (310) 539-5989
Retailer/Distributor

FOIE GRAS

WESTERN FOIE GRAS
DISTRIBUTING CO.
P.O. Box 5184, Santa Rosa, CA 95402
Tel: (707) 573-0728
Distributor

HUDSON VALLEY FOIE GRAS
80 Brooks Road
Ferndale, NY 12734
Tel: (914) 292-2500
Distributor

D'ARTAGNAN
280 Wilson Avenue
Newark, NJ 07105
Tel: (800) 327-8246
Website: www.dartagnan.com
Retailer/Distributor

QUINCE PASTE

THE SPANISH TABLE
1427 Western Avenue
Seattle, WA 98101
Tel: (206) 682-2827
E-mail: tablespan@aol.com

JUNE TAYLOR BAKING CO.
424 62nd Street
Oakland, CA 94609
Tel: (510) 653-2796

BLOOD SAUSAGE

MADE IN FRANCE
1301 Sixth Street, Suite F
San Francisco, CA 94107
Tel: (800) 464-6373
Fax: (415) 487-1101
Distributor

MARCEL & HENRI
415 Browning Way
South San Francisco, CA 94080
Tel: Outside California:
(800) 227-6436
California: (800) 542-4230
Retailer/Distributor

D'ARTAGNAN
280 Wilson Avenue
Newark, NJ 07105
Tel: (800) 327-8246
Website: www.dartagnan.com

TRUFFLES

MADE IN FRANCE
1301 Sixth Street, Suite F
San Francisco, CA 94107
Tel: (800) 464-6373
Fax: (415) 487-1101
Distributor

DEAN & DELUCA
560 Broadway, New York, NY 10012
Tel: (800) 999-0306
Fax: (212) 226-2003
Catalog: (800) 221-7714
Retail Stores in New York; California; Washington, D.C.; North Carolina; Missouri.

SHEET GELATIN

MADE IN FRANCE
1301 Sixth Street, Suite F
San Francisco, CA 94107
Tel: (800) 464-6373
Fax: (415) 487-1101
Distributor

VENISON AND OTHER GAME MEATS

D'ARTAGNAN
280 Wilson Avenue
Newark, NJ 07105
Tel: (800) 327-8246
Website: www.dartagnan.com
Retailer/Wholesaler

WHOLE FOODS MARKETS
Whole Foods Markets (Nationwide)
Website: www.wholefoods.com
Retailer

VERJUS

FUSION FOODS
P.O. Box 542, Rutherford, CA 94573
Tel: (800) 297-0686
Retailer/Distributor

DEAN & DELUCA
560 Broadway, New York, NY 10012
Tel: (800) 999-0306
Fax: (212) 226-2003
Catalog: (800) 221-7714
*Retail Stores in New York; California;
Washington, D.C.; North Carolina;
Missouri.*

TURRON

LA ESPAÑOLA MEATS, INC.
25020 Doble Avenue
Harbor City, CA 90710
Tel: (310) 539-0455
Fax: (310) 539-5989
Retailer/Distributor

THE SPANISH TABLE
1427 Western Avenue
Seattle, WA 98101
Tel: (206) 682-2827
E-mail: tablespan@aol.com

VEAL STOCK

MORE THAN GOURMET
(DEMI-GLACE GOLD)
115 West Bartges Street
Akron, OH 44311
Tel: (800) 860-9385
Retailer/Distributor

MADE IN FRANCE
1301 Sixth Street, Suite F
San Francisco, CA 94107
Tel: (800) 464-6373
Fax: (415) 487-1101

WHOLE FOODS MARKETS
(NATIONWIDE)
Website: www.wholefoods.com

WINES AND SPIRITS

PATXARAN

CHRISSA IMPORTS
280 Harbor Way
South San Francisco, CA 94080
Tel: (650) 877-8460

BASQUE WINES

KERMIT LYNCH WINE MERCHANT
(Domaine Arretxea and Etxegaraya
Irouleguys)
1605 San Pablo Avenue
Berkeley, CA 94702
Tel: (510) 524-1524

ASSOCIATED WINE DISTRIBUTING
(Txomin Etxaniz Txakoli, Remel-
luri Rioja)
P.O. Box 452, St. Helena, CA 94574
Tel: (707) 963-8055

CHRISSA IMPORTS
(Domaine Mignaberry Irouleguy,
Xuri D'Ansa Irouleguy)
280 Harbor Way
South San Francisco, CA 94080
Tel: (650) 877-8460

SOUTHERN WINE & SPIRITS OF
NORTHERN CALIFORNIA
(Marques de Riscal, Poire William)
33321 Dowe Avenue
Union City, CA 94587
Tel: (800) 548-3332

WINE TRADITIONS
(Domaine Brana, Domaine Ilaria)
6618 Tansey Drive
Falls Church, VA 22042
Tel: (703) 534-3430

YOUNG'S MARKETS
30740 Santana Street
Hayward CA 94544
Tel: (510) 475-2250

BASQUE LINENS/
TABLEWARE

JAN DE LUZ
P.O. Box 1115, Carmel, CA 93921
Tel: (831) 622-7621
Fax: (831) 622-7250
E-mail: jandeluz@aol.com

THE SPANISH TABLE
1427 Western Avenue
Seattle, WA 98101
Tel: (206) 682-2827
E-mail: tablespan@aol.com

Basque people (*cont.*)
  character of, 3
  community-based democracy of, 3
  as fishermen, 3, 9, 11, 19, 97, 100
  flag of, 7–8, 72, 98
  "houses" of, 3
  hunting of, 125, 127, 130, 132
  independence movement of, 2, 6–9
  origin of, 2–3
  political unity of, 3
  Roman relations with, 3
  sayings of, 1, 2
  as sheepherders, 6, 9–10, 37, 138, 142
  smuggling of, 110
  stories of, 3, 127, 152
Basse Navarre, 4, 6, 243
  cidrerie in, 184, 243
  restaurants in, 86, 96, 241
  wine of, 99
  see also St.-Jean-Pied-de-Port
basurdekumea saltsan (civet of wild boar), 130–31
Batua (unified Basque dialect), 5
Bayonnais, blueberry, 201
Bayonne, 241–44
  chocolate in, 11, 12, 196, 242
  Izarra distillery in, 219, 243
  restaurants in, 241
Bayonne ham:
  about, 10–11, 17
  Basque omelet with, 40–41
  in garbure, 29
  green peas with, 174
  in new potato and Romano bean ragout, 167
  and sheep's milk cheese terrine, 58–59
  sources of, 243, 245
  in stuffed squid in ink sauce, 80–81
  veal loin with sheep's milk cheese and, 156–58
bean(s):
  dried, preparation of, 178

fava, gratin, 171, 175
  grown among corn, 178
  Romano, and new potato ragout, 167
  see also garbanzo bean(s); white bean(s)
beef, 144–47
  cross rib with anchovy butter, grilled, 146–47
  short ribs with roasted beets in red wine sauce, 144–45
beet leaf fritters, 162–63
beets, roasted, beef short ribs in red wine sauce with, 144–45
begi-haundi eta almenzel limoi gurinarekin (cuttlefish steak with almond and lemon butter, 78–79
beignets, orange blossom, 202–3
bell peppers, red:
  and onion confit, 173
  roasted, in Idiazabal and mixed pepper croustade, 44–45
  roasted, sea scallop sauté with artichokes and, 108
  roasted, soup, 33
  roasted, stuffed with salt cod, 86–87
  sabayon, baked salmon fillet with, 100–101
  in veal stew, 159
  see also pimiento del piquillo de Lodosa
beltaraba ostozko kruspetak (beet leaf fritters), 162–63
Berasategui, Martin, 15, 242
beret Basque au chocolat, 194–95
berries, warm, cornmeal cake with, 184–85
bertsolari (troubadour), 12
Biarritz, 1, 6, 36, 186, 241–44
  bookshop in, 26
  chocolate in, 242
  Patisserie Dodin in, 194
  restaurants in, 62, 241
Bidart, 186
Bilbao, 5, 6, 7, 14

market in, 244
  restaurants in, 242
bildotxa intxaurrekin (lamb stew with mixed nut pesto), 140–41
biper erreak (roasted peppers), 233
biper erreta salda (roasted bell pepper soup), 33
biperrada (pipérade), 46
biperrak eta baba txuri gratin (piquillo pepper, rosemary, and white bean gratin), 57
biperrak makallaoz beteta (peppers stuffed with salt cod), 86–87
Biriatou, 150
Biscay, *see* Vizcaya
Biscay, Bay of, 4, 11, 238
bisque, crab, with brandy, 30
Bistrot Bellevue, 241
black sauce, 98
blood sausage:
  with cabbage and apple, 150
  sources of, 246
blueberry(ies):
  Bayonnais, 201
  in cornmeal cake with warm berries, 184–85
boar, wild, 132
  civet of, 130–31
bouquet garni, 16
braised veal sweetbreads in port wine sauce, 154–55
Brana, Jean, 222
Brana, Martine, 222
brandy:
  chocolate truffles with, 197
  crab bisque with, 30
  in Poire William sorbet, 222
bread:
  corn galettes, 234–35
  country, and cabbage soup gratinée (surfers' soup), 36
brioche, Basque, 204
bullfights, 144
butchering, 154
butter:
  almond and lemon cuttlefish steak with, 78–79

anchovy, grilled beef cross rib
with, 146–47
butter cream and almond meringue
cake, 182–83
butternut squash, *see* squash, butternut

cabbage:
blood sausage with apple and, 150
and country bread soup gratinée
(surfers' soup), 36
in garbure, 28–29
Café Iruna, 242
cakes, 181–88
almond meringue and butter
cream, 182–83
baked chocolate, 196
beret Basque au chocolat, 194–95
cornmeal, with warm berries,
184–85
gâteau Basque, 186–88
quince and goat cheese layer,
with candied pine nuts,
190–91
calamari, *see* squid
California, 136
see also San Francisco, Calif.
Cambo-les-Bains, 201, 241
Campagne et Gourmandises, 241
Campezo, 50
Cantabrian Mountains, 3, 140
caramel(ized):
and chestnut custard, 208
figs, goat's milk custard with
honey and, 212
quail, 125
Carlist Wars, 6
Carnival, 202, 209
Carrero Blanco, Luis, 8
carving, 119
Casa Nicolasa, 241
Castile, 4
caul fat, in roasted lamb loin with
garlic and thyme, 136–37
cèpes, sole braised with *txakoli* and,
94–95

chanterelles, breast of turkey stuffed
with chestnuts and, 116–17
Charlemagne, 4
Charles VII, King of France, 4
Chartreuse ice cream, 219
cheese:
cow's milk, 20–21
sources of, 242–43, 245
see also goat cheese; sheep's milk
cheese; *specific cheeses*
cherries:
dried, roasted duck with pine
nuts and, 121
festival of, 214
in red wine soup, 214–15
cherry preserves:
in fruit and cheese platter, 217
in gâteau Basque, 186
recipe for, 238
chestnut(s), 10, 11
breast of turkey stuffed with
chanterelles and, 116–17
butternut squash soup with
sheep's milk cheese and, 24
and caramel custard, 208
roasted, 236
soup with sautéed apple, 25
chicken:
carving of, 119
"Irouleguy," roasted, 118–19
poulet basquaise, 16, 120
chicken stock:
recipe for, 230
in soups, 24–27, 33
chile, Anaheim, *see* Anaheim chile(s)
chili powder, 18
Chilo, Pierre, 15, 241
chocolate, 181, 192–97
of Bayonne, 11, 12, 196, 242
beret Basque au chocolat, 194–95
cake, baked, 196
in civet of wild boar, 130–31
meringue *makilas* dipped in,
198–99
rocks, 192–93
sources of, 242
truffles with brandy, 197

chorizo:
about, 17–18
in ladies' rice, 151
in new potato and Romano bean
ragout, 167
and potato tortilla, 43
sources of, 246
Christmas, 93
Chueka, Ernesto, 94
Ciboure, 32, 244
cider, 11, 13, 148
pork roast, apple, 148–49
cidreries, 243
food served at, 146, 148, 184
civet of wild boar, 130–31
clams:
braised with halibut in green pea
salsa, 98
cherrystone, with garlic and parsley, 106
in hake San Sebastián style,
90–91
cod, fresh:
with Basquaise sauce, 89
rock, in fish cake Juan Mari,
82–83
rock, San Sebastián style,
90–91
cod, salt, 9
about, 19–20
"al pil-pil," 88
in leek and potato soup, 31
peppers stuffed with, 86–87
and potato salad, warm, 84
confit:
duck, 231
duck leg, 124
onion and pepper, 136–37, 173
pork, 152
tuna, 68
Confrèrie de la Garbure (Brotherhood
of Vegetable Soup), 28
cookies, 181, 198–200
almond (from gâteau Basque
dough), 188
almond macaroons, 200
meringue *makilas,* 198–99

Karlos Arguinano, 242

kauserak liranja liliekin (orange blossom beignets), 202–3

koka (crème caramel), 207

kremazko xigorrak (fried cream squares), 209

kuiatxoak (zucchini à la minute), 165

Labourd, 4, 5, 6, 188, 241–44
    cherries in, 238
    restaurants in, 1, 15, 62, 100, 107, 112, 241
    see also Espelette; Itxassou

La Concha, sea bream with garlic vinaigrette à, 92–93

ladies' rice, 151

La Goulue, calamari à, 62, 241

Laguardia, 170, 243

lamb, 136–43
    in blood sausage, 150
    chops Basquaise, barbecued, 138
    loin with garlic and thyme, roasted, 136–37
    shoulder with olive puree and ground almond powder, rolled, 142–43
    stew with mixed nut pesto, 140–41
    "*zikiro*," leg of, 139

Lapuyade, Henri, 150

La Rotonde, 241

Larressore, 198

Lasse, 184, 243

La Table des Frères Ibarboure, 15, 241

leche frita (fried cream squares), 209

Le Cheval Blanc, 241

leek(s):
    monkfish in red wine with pancetta and, 99
    and potato soup, 31

legatza koxkera (hake San Sebastián style), 90–91

leka eta pikuen entsalada intxaur olio-ozpinetan (*haricots verts* salad with figs and walnut vinaigrette), 70–71

Le Kaiku, 107, 241

lemon:
    and almond butter, cuttlefish steak with, 78–79
    sautéed prawns in pastis with cherry tomatoes and, 110–11

lemon zest, roasted potato salad with fresh herbs and, 74–75

Le Moulin d'Alotz, 241

Lent, 152, 177

lentils, green:
    with bacon, 176
    seared ahi tuna steaks with onion marmalade and, 102–3

Le Puy lentils, 176

Les Platanes, 241

linens, sources of, 244, 247

Linxe, Robert, 197

liqueur:
    in green apple sorbet, 220–21
    in Izarra ice cream, 219
    in Patxaran sorbet, 223
    in *turron* parfait, 224–25

Liquor de Manzana, in green apple sorbet, 221

liver:
    pâté, country-style, 60
    rabbit, 129
    see also foie gras

lobster, tomato gazpacho with, 34–35

Lodosa, 15
    see also pimento del piquillo de Lodosa

lodozakoak eta baratxuri frijitu ozpinarekin (roasted *piquillo* peppers with fried garlic vinaigrette), 48

Lorda, Jean Baptiste (partner), 110

Loti, Pierre, 16

Loustau, Jean-Guy, 105

lupia guzti erreta (whole roasted sea bass), 105

lursagar ahia (creamy mashed potatoes), 169

lursagar berri eta babarrun saltsa (new potato and Romano bean ragout), 167

lursagar erretak eta limoi entsalada (roasted potato salad with

lemon zest and fresh herbs), 74–75

lursagar eta babarruntxuri salda oliba (potato and white bean soup with olive puree), 32

lursagar gorri saltsa (potatoes Riojanas), 170

lursagar opila ardi-gasnarekin (Basque cheese and potato cakes), 172–73

lursagarrak baratxuriarekin (fried garlic potatoes), 168

macaroons, almond, 200

Magellan, Ferdinand, 47

magret of duck salad with apple and pomegranate, 122–23

mail-order sources, 245–47

Maison Adam, 200, 242

Maison du Chocolat, 197

makallaoa pil-pilean (salt cod "al pil-pil"), 88

makilak xokolaterekin (meringue *makilas*), 198–99

makilas, meringue, 198–99

makilas (Basque walking sticks), 198, 243

mamia piku eta eztiarekin (goat's milk custard with caramelized figs and honey), 212

Marcel & Henri, 150

Marichular, Vincent, 242

marinated:
    anchovies, 65
    barbecued lamb chops Basquaise, 138
    civet of wild boar, 130–31
    leg of lamb "*zikiro*," 139
    salmis of squab in red wine, 126–28
    tomato, onion, and pepper salad, 72

markets, 54, 244
    in San Sebastián, 1–2, 65, 82, 244

marmalade, onion, seared ahi tuna steaks with, 102–3

marmita (type of pot), 104

vinaigrette (*cont.*)
walnut, haricots verts salad
with figs and, 70–71
Vizcaya (Biscay), 4–7
restaurants in, 242
see also Bilbao; Santurce

walking sticks (*makilas*), 198, 243
walnut(s):
cream, 213
in lamb stew with mixed nut
pesto, 140–41
and sheep's milk cheese gratin,
216
vinaigrette, haricots verts salad
with figs and, 70–71
wee hours soup (garlic and egg), 37
Wells, Patricia, 26
whaling, 9, 19
white bean(s):

in garbure, 28–29
navy, 178
piquillo pepper, and rosemary
gratin, 57
and potato soup with olive puree,
32
white sauce, 98
wine, 11
sources of, 243, 247
see also port wine; red wine; *txakoli*
wineries, 94, 140, 162, 170, 243
witches, 139

Xabier (author's friend), 12
xardinak (sardines), 66
Xixtaberri—A Farm-Auberge in the
Country, 201, 241
xokolate boilak brandireki (chocolate
truffles with brandy), 197

Zagarramurdi, witches of, 139
zainzuri eta grisola beltza arroltzemoleta
(asparagus and black truffle
omelet), 42
zainzuri txuri entsalada (white asparagus salad), 73
*zapo ardo beltzean porru eta hirugihar-
rarekin* (monkfish in red wine
with leeks and pancetta), 99
"*zikiro*," leg of lamb, 139
Zortziko, 242
Zuberoa, 15, 26, 242
zucchini à la minute, 165